AF540771

age of

ANXIETY

age of ANXIETY

AMRITA TRIPATHI

KAMNA CHHIBBER

SIMON &
SCHUSTER

London • New York • Sydney • Toronto • New Delhi

First published in India by Simon & Schuster India, 2021

3 5 7 9 10 8 6 4 2

Simon & Schuster India
818, Indraprakash Building,
21, Barakhamba Road,
New Delhi 110001

www.simonandschuster.co.in

Paperback ISBN: 978-81-950571-6-0
eBook ISBN: 78-81-950571-7-7

Typeset in India by Mridu Agarwal, Simon & Schuster, New Delhi

Printed and bound in India by Replika Press Pvt. Ltd.

CONTENTS

FOREWORD BY DR ACHAL BHAGAT

It is the month of January of 2021. I am waiting in front of a booth in my hospital to get vaccinated, with a sense of trepidation. I am reflecting back on what a year 2020 has been. A year of worry, uncertainty, anticipation, avoidance and performing safety behaviours. One has walked through the year as an automaton and developed a hunchback peering into Zoom meeting screens. Yet, one has forced oneself to be reflective and hopeful. What a year! So, I write this in an unprocessed state of emotions.

While I am sitting here, I am also wondering what my mother would have felt if she had to live through 2020. It would have been quite a task for her to have lived through the last year.

I grew up in a home where anxiety was all-pervasive. My mother would have new physical symptoms which could not be explained and all of us would be concerned. The whole family would go to an uncle who was a physician. He would be reassuring or dismissive, depending perhaps on how his day had been. He would give some medicines. Some part of the prescription remained the same. There was an anti-allergy medicine, some paracetamol, and for a good measure, some homeopathic medicine. This ritual went on for years without a diagnosis of Anxiety or any other psychiatric disorder. So, yes, the last year would have been a tsunami for her. Even when I hypothetically consider this, I become worried.

In hindsight, I can now say that a diagnosis of my mother's difficulties would have been helpful, but it might still not have been a solution for her anxiety.

Is the experience of anxiety the same as the diagnosis of Anxiety? Can the narrative of a person who has lived through anxiety, with or without being diagnosed to have Anxiety, be explained by a checklist of Anxiety symptoms? Am I an anxious person? I have definitely experienced anxiety in the last year, and in the years before. Will I meet the criteria of the diagnosis of Anxiety? Maybe. Perhaps not.

The experience of anxiety is universal. Most of us experience anxiety, but may not reach the threshold of a diagnosis. The diagnosis of Anxiety is meant to be more specific. The diagnosis is more measurable. It makes a sub-group of people to be easily recognised as having Anxiety. Then there is what clinicians like me call co-morbidity. However, the lived experience of anxiety is not a mutually exclusive category; there are overlaps in life. Depression, Anxiety or Adjustment Disorders are good categories for research, but mostly co-exist in life. Life is more of a matrix than we clinicians make it seem.

In my experience, we need to move from treatments to solutions and that will happen only when diagnosis and experience inform our practice. Solutions do not ignore people's agency, treatments sometimes do. In an effort to be standardised and 'evidence based', we sometimes ignore the reality that everyone will evolve their own solution. At the same time, in the name of 'eclectic' and 'personalised,' what sometimes get peddled could be downright harmful. People need information to make choices.

This effort of *The Health Collective*, hopefully, would help people make informed choices. Like their earlier publication, this book by *The Health Collective* talks about a continuum: a bridge across the dichotomies of diagnosis and experience. While it takes us on a journey of memories, smells and images through people's personal stories, it also talks about 'stepped care models', symptoms and treatments. I hope it is read by clinicians as a textbook. And I hope it is read by everyone as a book of hope and recovery.

Do not fall for the dichotomy of fear and anxiety which most 'frequently asked questions' trying to explain Anxiety start with. There is a lot that lies in between. Your anxiety is real and it need not always be diagnosable. Your anxiety cannot be compared to someone else's anxiety and diminished. Your anxiety can be helped. There is a solution there. Look after yourself. Take care!

Dr Achal Bhagat
January 2021

INTRODUCTION

Amrita Tripathi

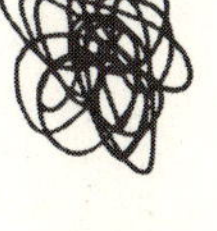

I started working on issues to do with mental health and illness as a reporter more than a decade and a half ago — not very regularly back then, but each story made me learn something new and startling (for example, when I learned that the way we report on suicide and suicide prevention can actually either do so much catastrophic harm or be a force for good, or again when I discovered through an interview with a child and adolescent psychiatrists that kids as young as 11/12 years of age were coming in worried they were pregnant, while schools, educators and parents quibbled about whether to include sex education in the curriculum!)

In 2016, I set up a site called *The Health Collective*, to help raise awareness about mental health and mental illness in India, by sharing stories, to help tackle the stigma together (and individually). People shared their stories bravely (and it is something that takes a tremendous amount of courage, even in privileged India today) and many of the stories of lived experience resonated with others, and slowly, we realised there was a community here, a tribe, even.

We have about 300 stories up on the site, including first person stories of lived experience, comics, columns and helpful articles and video interviews with leading psychiatrists like Dr Achal Bhagat and psychologists like my wonderful co-author Kamna Chhibber. Whereas today in 2021, there's no dearth of video sessions, webinars, Insta influencers, and celebrities sharing their stories, and more than enough pop psychology doing the rounds, I've never lost sight of that original mission, which is to raise awareness, help tackle stigma, and to do this all from an India lens, while creating a safe space.

Easier said than done, I realise. But we hope that you — the reader — will join us in that mission because we do need each one of us to play a part.

So we return to story-telling. The Mindscape series of books, commissioned by Simon and Schuster India, originated in conversations I had with Himanjali Sankar, my editor, on the need to have more stories told from an Indian point of view. We rely on people to share from their own journeys, and we want to present these to you, as they do, in the hope that this will make your journey easier. Whatever you, or a loved one, might be going through, you're not alone.

While I have learned much along the way, including the fact that there is no one-size-fits-all model, I have learned that there are a few themes that come up often. For those of us who think somehow we're immune, that anxiety won't affect us, I'm afraid that this is a myth (as Tanmoy Goswami spells out in his interview).

For those of us who think that stigma is a thing of the past, or that anxiety is like 'nervousness' or all in your head, it's worth reading Ayushi Khemka's story and description of it as a 'tear-inducing, panic-striking, body-trembling, mind-numbing condition far removed from the "pastel aesthetics" favoured by brands and influencers. Rajashree Gandhi writes of Anxiety feeling "like a bunch of voices speaking in a loud volume at the same time", even as she shares something that helped her, namely, the bullet journal.

Our attempt here is to sift through the cacophony, to help elevate some of the conversations, and voices that can help us all make sense of what it means to have Anxiety in India. For those of us who feel that we don't have the skill set to make a difference, we can equip ourselves with the basics (as you'll hear from Dr Soumitra Pathare in his interview, on the importance of a stepped care approach) — the bottom line is that we can each of us learn to listen with empathy, without judgement. We can also learn when to help guide someone to a professional for help, if they need it. I suppose these are lessons that can come in handy, no matter what walk of life you're in. And they will come into play again and again, in your personal life.

As with our previous titles in the Mindscape series, *Real Stories of Dealing with Depression* (co-authored with psychologist Arpita Anand) and *Young Mental Health* (co-authored with psychologist Meera Haran Alva), this book is meant to help start conversations. It's also intended to be an easier read than you might think — we'll dial back the jargon, and keep it as reader-friendly as possible, without losing out on the nuance.

We are centering stories of lived experience, as perhaps no one can explain what it means to have Anxiety or live with an Anxiety Disorder as well as those who are living and dealing with it. We are including interviews with experts, who also share from their own personal journeys and I'm delighted to have some creative writing in here as well, through which you may find an insightful

entry point into understanding what it is like to deal with Anxiety.

We are sharing Common Myths and Facts, colloquial ways of talking about Anxiety, Tips on Self-Care and where to get help, Covid-19 and Anxiety and why we can call this the Age of Anxiety (perhaps tongue-in-cheek because it's also quite an over-used expression!)

When we use Anxiety with a capital A, that's for the disorder, whereas as you'll hear from Kamna and from Dr Soumitra Pathare, we all use anxiety as laypeople, as a very 'normal' response to stressors. ('Normal' in quotes because that's a whole different conversation.)

My hope with this entire ambitious *Mindscape* endeavour is that we can help move the needle on the conversations around Mental Health in this country, that we can learn to be kinder about difficult conditions and conversations, with each other and ourselves, and that we can learn that we're not walking alone. There are many survivors, mental health advocates and champions, and people doing extraordinary things, who would want you, the reader, to know that you're not alone. Again, easier said than lived, and we don't mean that it's going to be easy or a walk in the park (far from it!) but ... hopefully hearing from others who are going through their own journeys and sharing what they think might be helpful, can make a difference.

I want to thank each of our contributors, and this is not an exhaustive summary of 'What it means to have Anxiety in India', nor is it a prescriptive book by any stretch, and as always, I wish it could be as inclusive as possible. We can always do more, do better. It's been an ambitious (and even audacious) series of books, not to mention project overall, but we hope that it helps to make a difference (however small). You — dear reader — are more than welcome to reach out to us (team@healthcollective.in) to comment, or to feature any of your work on our site and future iterations ... I hope this is helpful, and that it is a good read.

As Dr Bhagat writes in the foreword, your anxiety cannot be compared to someone else's and it shouldn't be diminished. It can be helped.

A note on the structure: These should work as stand-alone chapters. I don't recommend trying to read this book cover to cover! Much like *Young Mental Health* and *Real Stories* ... you can dip in, take a pause, make notes and come back to it later.

There is no *You Should/ You Must/ You Shouldn't* here — do take what's useful for you and those you care about. Here's to more conversations!

INTRODUCTION

Kamna Chhibber

In my clinical practice over the years, the number of people who would come in to my therapy chamber complaining of 'having Anxiety' has seen a rise. I have heard statements like '*You have no idea how anxious I am*', '*I may look fine to you but inside I'm just so nervi, all up in knots, all the time*', '*There is so much that keeps running in my head I struggle to keep the noise down*', '*My stomach keeps churning so often. Small things become real big triggers*'.

In recent years, as the discourse on mental health has expanded, people have become aware of what mental health is, how mental health-related illnesses manifest and the impact they can have, along with an understanding of the importance and effectiveness of treatments. However, concurrently, what has also increased is the number of people who may mislabel what they are experiencing as Anxiety.

The term has entered our everyday language where saying '*I'm stressed*' or '*I'm anxious*' is the norm. From a school-going child to an elderly individual, anyone could identify themselves as being anxious. Their reasons do, of course, vary. The triggers for each tend to be different. The manifestation can also be variable. What is also seen is that almost anything can contribute towards making people feel this 'anxious state'. The most innocuous situations from within a person's environment and life can lead to the resultant label of being anxious or worried.

The question that arises at this juncture is '*Is this really Anxiety?*'

What mental health experts would refer to and label as Anxiety, the clinical condition with varying manifestations in the form of generalised anxiety disorder, panic disorder, specific phobia, selective mutism, separation anxiety disorder, social anxiety disorder, agoraphobia, are in fact different from what lay people would experience anxiety to be.

For us (mental health professionals), Anxiety is not just about feeling worried, having more thoughts in the mind, feeling worked up about something 'bad' that happened during the day, or losing a couple of nights' sleep over something.

Anxiety as a clinical condition, which encompasses the above mentioned conditions, which we would be exploring through the course of this book includes features of excessive fear, anxiousness and related behavioural disturbances. It can also involve experiencing significant physical symptoms that relate to feeling anxious. These symptoms and the effects of the problem last for specific periods of time which are critical to the reaching of the diagnosis. An additional element that is of great importance is the extent to which the individual's symptoms are interfering with their functioning across different domains specific to their life, such as their profession or occupation, their social relationships and their personal relationships, to name a few.

It is through a comprehensive understanding of these varying numerous aspects that a diagnosis is arrived at and a decision is made about which approach to treatment would be best suited for the specific individual. There is no one-size-fits-all solution that is available when it comes to mental health illnesses and this includes Anxiety disorders as well. Determining an approach is contingent upon numerous factors. We would be exploring and understanding how you reach this approach which would be most beneficial for you.

This is not to say that there are no general strategies that can support you in containing your general anxiousness, even if it emerges in moments and not as a part of a larger illness. We would, across the pages of the book, also be exploring these strategies which can be integrated into your daily routine and practices, ways of approaching situations and problems, thinking through the decisions and choices you need to make and the coping mechanisms you can explore. These individually and also as a cumulative approach can be beneficial in helping you cope with the anxiousness that can take root in different moments of your life.

Finally, through the medium of this book we do aim to dismiss the various misconceptions that surround Anxiety. We also purport to help you differentiate your feeling of anxiousness, which is an adaptive response ensuring our survival as a species, from the Anxiety that is an illness and requires intervention from an expert. In doing so, we look to provide a roadmap for an approach that you or anyone you know, can take in order to determine when you need to seek help and when it is that you can work on it yourself through the suggested mechanisms.

Mental health illnesses need not be feared. They can be mitigated and resolved. This is the foundation of the approach we envisage here in this book. Everything thereafter is built upon this premise, which, if embraced, can enable the activation of an adaptive coping response on your part.

COMMON COLLOQUIAL TERMS USED TO DESCRIBE ANXIETY[1]

- Tension

Hindi:

- *Ghabrahat, bechaini, darr*
- *Niraashapan*
- *Udaasi*
- *Mann nahin lagna/ Mann Nahin lag raha hai*
- *Chinta*
- *Hudhud*
- *Kaalji*
- *Baar baar rona aata hai*
- *Kisi cheez main dhyaan nahin lagta*
- *Mann ashaant hai*
- *Chidchidahat hota hai*
- *Saans phoolti hai*
- *Bechaini lagti hai*
- *Chakkar aata hai*
- *Sar bhaari hai/ Dil bhaari-bhaari hai*
- *Kuch acha nahi lagta*
- *Soch-vichaar aana*
- *Uljhan*
- *Neend mein bhi chinta lagi rehti hai*
- *Acha nahi lagna, nirasha, vait vatna*

PART ONE

WHAT IS ANXIETY?

Kamna Chhibber

Answering the question 'What is Anxiety?' is difficult. Every individual has their own conceptualisation of what it means to be anxious. Before we start delving into what it would mean to be anxious and having an Anxiety Disorder from a clinical perspective, let's start by asking our own selves this question.

Take a piece of paper and jot down for yourself what you understand anxiety to mean at this moment when you are reading this line. Also make a note of some of the situations where you think you feel anxious. You can use words or phrases or write full sentences or even a paragraph to make this note for yourself.

Now ensure you keep this paper with yourself. Don't lose it. We'll be using this paper/note later during the course of the book as you navigate its different parts. You can also use the blank side on the following page to make this note for yourself.

We also asked a few people we know to share their initial first thoughts with us on how they conceptualise anxiety. We are keeping their responses anonymous as per their request. Here are a few of the responses that we received:

For me anxiety is the absolute worst feeling. It is synonymous with being out of control of my body, and my mind. I fail to function when I get into anxious phases. And I have noticed once I do get anxious it stays with me for a while. This hasn't always been the case. And even now for me anxiety can happen for brief periods such as for a few minutes, or it can even, last up to hours and sometimes even go on to extend into days!

– 24-YEAR-OLD WOMAN, WORKING AT A COMPANY

Anxiety was when I used to give exams. I would have the worst feeling descend upon me like it was life or death. If I failed to perform it was as though the whole world would come crashing down and nothing could be fine after it. Obviously that was never the case. When things didn't go well nothing did come crashing down but that was — and even now in situations where I am being evaluated, is — the absolute worst I can feel.

– 35-YEAR-OLD MAN, BANKING EXECUTIVE

Anxiety has been my friend. I feel that when I have gotten anxious it actually helped me avert a bad situation. I don't know if that is all that good because people around me also complain that I am over-cautious. I do feel that to an extent I am like that. I do assess situations a lot more than others I know do and I can get stuck before I can take a decision but I can't always make up my mind on whether it is all good or all bad.

— 28-YEAR-OLD MAN, MANAGEMENT EXECUTIVE

When I get stressed, I start developing these aches and pains. My limbs hurt, sometimes my face and head. I have even had an upset stomach often times. And in general my stomach can be doing somersaults when I am anxious. It is the worst feeling ever and I do feel like I need immediate help at that time. It can get really bad for me.

— 39-YEAR-OLD WOMAN, IT PROFESSIONAL

When you consider all these descriptions, what is most evident is the underlying theme of experiencing physical symptoms which can potentially create extreme discomfort, as well as thoughts that can seem to spiral out of control. The situations are variable and different people can experience anxiety in different situations in the same way or even different ways.

If we were to try and define what Anxiety is, the following is a good way to conceptualise and understand it:

Anxiety is experienced by every individual. It is the anticipation of future threat. It is characterized most commonly as a diffuse, unpleasant, vague sense of apprehension, often accompanied by autonomic symptoms such as headache, perspiration, palpitations, tightness in the chest, mild stomach discomfort, and restlessness indicated by an inability to sit or stand still for long. The particular constellation of symptoms present during Anxiety tends to vary among persons.

— SADDOCK, SADDOCK & RUIZ[2] (2015)

Anxiety, in fact, acts like a signal that indicates to the individual the possibility of an impending danger. It allows people to be able to take precautions and instate measures to be able to deal with the threat effectively. It is different from the fear that can get triggered within you in the face of danger. Fear is an emotional response that occurs when there is a real, known, external, definite source of threat. In contrast, Anxiety is triggered in response to an anticipated, unknown and vague stimulus.

It is important to understand these subtle differences as they enable you to be able to label correctly what you are experiencing in a given situation. Often, individuals are in fact feeling fear in a real situation that they find themselves in, but mislabel it as Anxiety.

Our minds are trained to also look at Anxiety as a much 'bigger thing/experience' and one that is indicative of a possibly larger issue. This can make you feel even more excessively worried and trigger even more intense feelings of anxiousness within you.

Now go back to the note that you made about what Anxiety means to you and the situations you identified that make you feel anxious. Utilising your understanding of what Anxiety is, and how it can be differentiated from fear, reassess and re-evaluate whether what you have felt in these situations was Fear or Anxiety. This process of reappraising the emotions you have felt and the situations you have experienced will help you develop a better understanding of the anxiety you feel. When you are equipped with this knowledge you would feel empowered to change the narrative that runs in your mind about how you think and feel in situations. We would be exploring this more elaborately in the subsequent chapters.

We would now look at developing a better understanding of the kind of emotions you feel in situations before we go on to getting to know more about Anxiety Disorders.

Fear and Anxiety

Fear is an individual's response to a real threat within the environment. It is related to a known, definite, external source.

Anxiety is an alerting signal which warns an individual of impending danger or threat, enabling them to take measures in advance to deal with the threat.

UNDERSTANDING THE EMOTIONS YOU FEEL

People commonly experience a plethora of emotions across situations. It is important to be able to recognise, understand and remember the diverse emotional experiences that occur in given situations. For most, emotional vocabulary tends to be rather limited and there is a struggle to come up with precise words that can definitively indicate towards what one is feeling. Before we move forward, try this. Take a moment to reflect and consider the different words you use regularly to denote emotion. Make a list of these.

You are most likely to come up with a limited range of words that you typically use to express what you are feeling in situations. Mostly, you perhaps end up utilising words like sad, happy, angry, anxious, worried to refer to feeling states. Other emotional expressions such as disgust, guilt, disdain, despair, apprehension, may not often feature in the way you would describe your emotional state. Additionally, frequently people utilise expressions of physical experiences to indicate towards an emotional experience; such as when people refer to feeling tired.

Expanding your emotional vocabulary is a helpful starting point if you are looking towards building your emotional health. A limited vocabulary necessarily limits your ability to name and label your emotional experiences and thus even takes away from you being able to do something about it.

So what you can do is use the emotion chart provided on the next page as a ready reference to identify the emotion you are really experiencing. Also, remember that it is not black and white and you may end up identifying a few different words that more comprehensively describe how you feel.

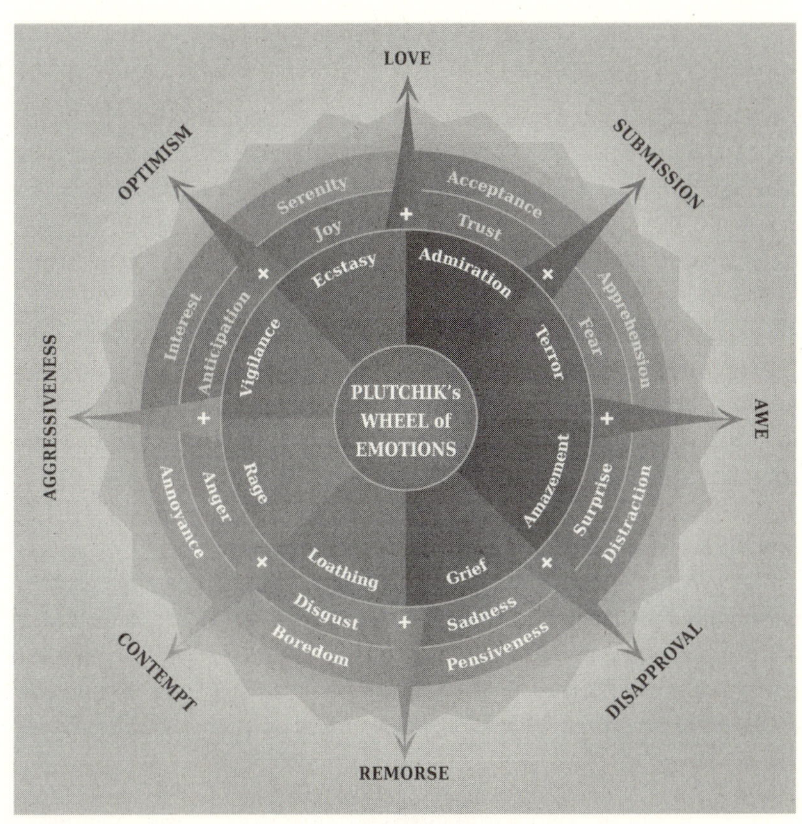
LOVE
OPTIMISM
SUBMISSION
AGGRESSIVENESS
AWE
CONTEMPT
DISAPPROVAL
REMORSE
Serenity
Acceptance
Joy
Trust
Ecstasy
Admiration
Interest
Anticipation
Vigilance
Apprehension
Fear
Terror
PLUTCHIK's
WHEEL of
EMOTIONS
Rage
Anger
Annoyance
Amazement
Surprise
Distraction
Loathing
Grief
Disgust
Sadness
Boredom
Pensiveness

MYTHS AND FACTS

Mental health related illnesses have long been plagued by many misconceptions and myths, which prevent people from talking about their experiences and seeking help from experts. The hesitation comes from the fear of not being understood, being misunderstood, misrepresented, judged or castigated for being weak or having deficient coping skills, that make it difficult to work through challenging circumstances.

Here are some more commonly held myths that are seen to be associated with Anxiety Disorders and which you must be aware of to ensure that they don't come in the way of seeking help and support for yourself or for those you know and love.

Myth: Stress and Anxiety Disorders are synonymous

Fact: When we specifically consider Anxiety Disorders, it is easy for people to feel confused about how it is different from the stress that can be experienced as one operates across different spaces. Stress happens in response to specific external triggers or situations which can be present in the short term or even long term. People can experience physical discomfort, emotional upheaval or psycho-

logical distress on account of the stressors in their lives. However, when there are persistent, excessive, intense worries that occur outside of the presence of a trigger or stressor in the environment and which create extreme discomfort for the individual it is termed as anxiety.

Myth: If I worry, it means I have an Anxiety Disorder

Fact: Worry is often used interchangeably with Anxiety though it bears significant differences from it. Worry is usually seen to be more related to what is happening in a person's mind, it is specific, can lead to mild distress, but is controllable and also can encourage problem solving as it is usually associated with more realistic situations. Anxiety in contrast is likely to lead to more intense, pervasive, difficult emotional, physiological and psychological experiences, tends to be more diffuse, leads to excessive distress, is less controllable and can relate to aspects that are not necessarily occurring in the present or at times not related to a real threat in the environment, thus lingering outside of the presence of a real situation.

Myth: If you have an Anxiety Disorder you must avoid situations that cause you to experience stress

Fact: The avoidance of situations or experiences that contribute towards your Anxiety contributes towards reinforcing it. It is a myth to believe that avoidance

would make the Anxiety manageable. In contrast, it tends to diminish your confidence and takes away from your ability to believe that you can work through a difficult situation. It is important to avoid the avoidance and develop healthy coping mechanisms that can allow you to work through the stressors and anxiety-provoking situations that you encounter.

Myth: The causes for Anxiety Disorders are rooted in childhood and so a focus needs to be on working through these

Fact: It is important to remember that there is a biopsychosocial explanation that provides an understanding of why people can develop an Anxiety Disorder. Keeping this in mind is important when understanding how the illness needs to be approached along with the treatment paradigms that are envisaged. Past experiences, particularly pertaining to childhood are not alone responsible for the precipitation of an Anxiety Disorder. Thus, treatment approaches do not always have to look at focusing on the past and would need to contribute towards what is happening in the present, the here-and-now of what an individual is going through.

ONE EMOTION: DIFFERENT TERMINOLOGIES

Look back at the page that starts this chapter. Numerous words can come to mind to signify the experience of being anxious.

Some utilise the description of physical sensations to guide the language they use to describe their experience, while others utilise words that indicate the thoughts that come to their mind when they feel anxious. For others, the description of how they experience Anxiety can be in the form of metaphors.

When we have spoken to people, they have used varying labels to describe what Anxiety means to them. The following are some commonly used phrases, which give an understanding of how vastly diverse the actual experience of Anxiety can be from one person to another:

- *Bechaini*
- *Ghabrahat*
- *Halkat*
- *Hararat*
- *Dum ghutna*
- *Atka hua mehsoos karna*
- *Bahut soch aana*
- *Kuch bura ho jayega*
- Nervousness
- Restlessness
- Fidgetiness
- Over-thinking
- Over-analysing

- Excessively preoccupied
- Clogged in the mind
- Unable to focus
- Feeling of impending doom

ANXIETY DISORDERS

We know that experiencing anxiety occasionally is a part of our lives and its presence in itself does not indicate a clinical problem that must be addressed. **However, when this Anxiety becomes pervasive, more intense with time and impedes functioning across the different roles and responsibilities that you might have, it requires attention.**

In such a situation you might feel out of control, find it difficult to maintain your focus or pay attention and also experience sudden episodes of intense fear or anxiousness, which we call panic attacks. This can also push you to want to avoid situations and places or experiences where you fear experiencing the Anxiety which adversely impacts the quality of the life that you lead.

In order to understand whether someone has an Anxiety Disorder or not, it is important to know some indicative symptoms. Please do not attempt to diagnose yourself, but do refer to a counsellor, or a trained therapist in case you are concerned.

Some commonly reported symptoms are below:

- Dizziness
- Headaches
- Nausea
- Feeling nervous
- Increased heart rate or palpitations
- Excessive sweating
- Clammy hands and feet
- Tremulousness
- Breathing quickly
- Feeling of danger or doom
- Difficulty in focusing
- Feeling tired
- Gastrointestinal difficulties
- Overthinking
- Difficulty controlling worry
- Getting lost in thoughts that circulate in the mind
- Avoidance of situations that contribute to Anxiety

What the presence of these kind of symptoms can do is impact your confidence and belief system in who you are and what you can do or achieve. Given that this Anxiety can arise unbidden and without a necessary trigger within the environment, the lack of predictability can make you more apprehensive and tentative in planning out things for yourself and making decisions as well. Its presence over extended durations of time can lead to dips in moods, an increase in irritability and also affect your productivity and relationships.

Anxiety Disorders include a varying range of conditions. These are as follows:

1. Generalised Anxiety Disorder – This condition includes excessive worry and anxiousness around a range of activities and experiences, including general routine activities. It tends to be pervasive and persistent, the worry being out of proportion to the situation, being difficult to control and affecting one in multiple ways.

2. Agoraphobia – In this condition a person has a fear of and often avoids being in large, open spaces that cause them to experience panic. They avoid being in such situations where a primary fear is being trapped or not being able to escape or experiencing embarrassment.

3. Panic Disorder – In this condition an individual experiences sudden feelings of intense anxiety and panic that reaches a peak within a few minutes. Typically the symptoms seen include feeling breathless, having palpitations, dizziness, nausea, impending sense of doom, shortness of breath, to name a few. It increases the worry about such events occurring in the future, enhancing the need to avoid being in them.

4. Social Anxiety Disorder – This condition involves intense anxiety and worry about being in social situations due to fears of being embarrassed, having to perform, being judged or feeling self-conscious.

5. Specific Phobias – A specific phobia involves an intensely anxious reaction to specific stimuli within the environment. It can also lead to the experience of panic attacks when faced with the phobic object or situation.

6. Selective Mutism – Seen in children, selective mutism is a condition in which a child fails to speak in certain situations even though (s)he has no specific speech related deficits per se. This can severely impede their functioning in school, at home or in social situations as well.

7. Separation Anxiety Disorder – This is a childhood Anxiety-related disorder in which a child experiences excessive Anxiety inappropriate to the age or developmental level when experiencing separation from parents or parental figures.

These Anxiety Disorders can and do severely impede the functioning of the individual in the varying areas of their functioning and can be debilitating for the person diagnosed with it.

As you'll read in the following chapters, through the essays and interviews describing different forms of Anxiety Disorders, they can be treated, once identified and addressed.

WHAT CAUSES ANXIETY DISORDERS

Like any other mental health-related illness, Anxiety Disorders too have a biopsychosocial cause that relates to their precipitation and prevalence.

People who develop an Anxiety Disorder are seen to have a biological predisposition to developing the illness which is mediated by the imbalance in neurotransmitters. Concurrently there are associated psychological aspects that play a contributory role towards the development of the illness.

These include factors like having a sensitive temperament or personality, being more reactive or having beliefs about the self or the world that contribute towards Anxiety and the kind of coping mechanisms that one possesses. Finally, social aspects such as how the individual's environment is, the social support they have in place, the role models they are surrounded by can play a substantial role as well.

PREVALENCE OF ANXIETY DISORDERS IN INDIA

Anxiety disorders are the second most common mental health-related illness which roughly affects 1 in 10 people in the world.

Whereas mental health illnesses in India are seen to have a life time prevalence rate of 13.7% as per the latest Mental Health Survey 2015–16,[3] phobic Anxiety Disorders were reported to affect 1.9% of the population. Other Anxiety disorders have been reported in the survey to affect approximately 1.3% of the population. In adolescents, the prevalence of Anxiety Disorders was reported to be at 3.6% of the population.

LIVING WITH AND UNDERSTANDING ANXIETY IN INDIA

Arti Malik

Arti Malik first shared a version of this chapter in a piece[4] *for* The Health Collective. *Arti Malik has worked in the field of development, law and human rights, specifically on the intersection of public health, education and vulnerable populations. She is a member of Volunteers Collective and one of the trustees of The Community Library Project. She grew up in Meerut (UP) and has lived in Delhi (more or less) since she moved here to attend college. She lives with Anxiety and for readers of this book, has shared more on what it feels like to have an Anxiety Disorder, as well as some common Myths and Facts.*

Most of us have experienced feelings of apprehension or physical unease, for example (and often) when we are faced with a difficult situation. We live in an environment that is dynamic and challenging in multiple ways and this can often lead to stress. While we tend to possess effective coping mechanisms to deal with everyday stress, sometimes these mechanisms can become over-activated, maladaptive, and can lead to Anxiety.

ANXIETY VS ANXIETY DISORDERS

Anxiety is a subjective feeling of being in a state of unease, apprehension, worry, fear or discomfort, often accompanied by physical symptoms such as heart palpitations, trembling, sweating, headache, etc. These are perfectly normal ways in which a person responds to a real or potential danger. However, if these feelings and physical symptoms occur for a prolonged period of time, or often in an extreme or disproportionate fashion that makes a person feel helpless and debilitated, then the person may be suffering from an Anxiety Disorder.

Anxiety Disorders are grouped as a range of mental disorders characterised by feelings of anxiety and fear. They include generalised anxiety disorder, social anxiety disorder, specific phobia, separation anxiety disorder, panic disorder, etc. (as you read in the previous section.)

Anxiety Disorders are among one of the most prevalent mental, emotional and behavioural problems in the world, estimated to affect 3.4% of the global population as of 2015, or about 264 million people, according to the World Health Organisation.[5]

They are and should be an important focus of research and an issue for public health as they seriously affect the quality of life of a person suffering from any of them and they pose a heavy cost burden in managing the disorders in patients.

Thirty-five-year-old Isha (name changed on request) suffers from social phobia, one of the most common Anxiety Disorders. She tells *The Health Collective* about her university days and early work life. 'I came across as shy or even arrogant sometimes, to most of my college-mates and colleagues. I had few friends and I was constantly overwhelmed by the thought of attending social events, parties and even extra-curricular activities involving a group of people, and chose to mostly excuse myself from them. On one hand I felt extremely lonely and on the other totally terrified by social situations.'

Even today, socialising can be an ordeal, but she is equipped with more knowledge about her condition. 'It is only after I began therapy in my late twenties that I realised I suffered from social phobia. It is easier now than before, but even now my automatic reaction to an invitation to socialise is a vehement no.'

PREVALENCE IN INDIA

Epidemiological studies and research, specifically on Anxiety Disorders has been inadequate in India. According to an article by Trivedi and Gupta[6] on the overview of Indian research on Anxiety Disorders, there is discrepancy on prevalence rates of Anxiety Disorders due to many reasons, including under-reporting, poor screening instruments, exclusion of certain Anxiety Disorders from the surveys, small sample size, etc.

The first ever nationwide survey on mental health covering 28 states in 2015–2016 gives us a better idea about the prevalence of Anxiety Disorders in India.

According to the National Mental Health Survey conducted by the National Institute of Mental Health and Neuro Sciences (NIMHANS),[7] the prevalence of Anxiety Disorders such as phobic disorders, agoraphobia, generalised anxiety disorder, obsessive compulsive disorder is higher in females than in males. Adolescents are also disproportionately affected with Anxiety Disorders as in many cases, symptoms of an Anxiety Disorder manifest themselves in early adolescence and may continue to persist throughout adulthood and old age. The survey also indicates that mental disorders including Anxiety Disorders affect the productive age group between 30 and 49 the most and peaks during this time.

A study conducted by 1to1help.net, a professional counselling company, reportedly found that 1 in every 2 employees in corporate jobs in India suffers from anxiety and depression, as reported by *The Deccan Chronicle.*[8]

SYMPTOMS, CAUSES AND MANAGEMENT

Physical sensations include headache, nausea, vomiting, sweating, trembling, stomach pain, tingling, weakness, body ache, feeling shortness of breath, hot flashes or chills, etc.

Emotional sensations include nervousness, fear, irritability, worry, insecurity, isolation from others, self-consciousness, desire to escape, etc. The effect of these symptoms leads to the impairment of cognitive processes such as thinking, decision-making ability, perception of the environment, learning ability, memory and concentration.

Persons suffering from an Anxiety Disorder, therefore, may find it difficult to carry out certain tasks or respond to certain situations in an appropriate manner.

Research shows that a variety of biological, psychological and social factors can contribute to Anxiety Disorders. Biological factors may include genes that may predispose certain people to Anxiety Disorders. Psychological factors may include behavioural factors where a person may develop a maladaptive learned response to specific past experiences and applies it to future similar situations. Social factors that can lead to Anxiety Disorders include life experiences such as death in a family, divorce, financial troubles, major illnesses, long term exposure to abuse, violence, etc.

To effectively diagnose and treat Anxiety Disorders, it is important to understand the underlying causes of the disorder.

Psychiatrist Dr Jai Meher from the Institute of Human Behaviour and Allied Sciences (IHBAS) tells *The Health Collective*, 'In my clinical practice, I have seen that often patients suffering from an anxiety disorder have maladaptive coping mechanisms formed in their childhood due to lack of appropriate parental guidance or neglect or other social, psychological or biological factors, which are difficult to shake off in adulthood. Therefore in treating and managing Anxiety, the importance in therapy should be given to learning new coping mechanisms and that can take time and patience.'

DIAGNOSIS AND MANAGEMENT OF ANXIETY DISORDERS

Diagnosis and management of Anxiety Disorders in India can be challenging for a number of reasons:

- Mental disorders in general still carry a lot of stigma attached to them in India and thus can lead to neglect and marginalisation.
- Particularly because of their subjective nature, Anxiety Disorders can further lead to more neglect. A person suffering from an Anxiety Disorder may not be able to comprehend their feelings and in turn may not be able to communicate to others what they are experiencing.
- Lack of awareness regarding Anxiety Disorders can also hinder one's ability to seek help.
- Research and epidemiological studies on mental disorders have neglected Anxiety Disorders in India for a long time, which affects the diagnosis, treatment and management of Anxiety Disorders.
- The abysmal mental health care system in India and its high costs invariably come in the way of persons seeking help, especially if they belong to rural, low-income, marginalised and vulnerable groups.

MANAGEMENT/ TREATMENT

Once diagnosed, Anxiety Disorders can be treated in a number of ways:

- **Anti-anxiety medication** may be prescribed to relieve physical and emotional symptoms.
- **Cognitive behavioural therapy** and/or other psychotherapies address underlying issues, coping mechanisms and responses of a person, which may help in

managing Anxiety and its symptoms.

• Learning **relaxation and stress management techniques** and exercises such as mindfulness and yoga can be beneficial in the long term management of Anxiety.

CHALLENGES: WHAT INDIA NEEDS

Despite availability of medication, therapy and other techniques that can significantly reduce the discomfort and debilitation associated with Anxiety Disorders and help people lead more productive and healthier lives, most persons suffering from Anxiety Disorders are not able to seek appropriate treatment and care.

One of the first steps towards addressing Anxiety Disorders in India would be to create awareness among people of all ages and among all populations. Improving access and affordability to mental health care would encourage more people to seek help. Moreover, focused research on the social and cultural aspects in specific contexts of the population in India would help in determining the causes and perhaps designing interventions to adequately address the problem of Anxiety Disorders in India.

1. WHAT DOES IT FEEL LIKE TO HAVE ANXIETY?

When I get anxious, I start to feel physically uncomfortable, heart palpitating, restlessness, a gnawing feeling that something is amiss, a feeling of dread and impending doom and of being out of control. These feelings can persist over hours and days on and off, and can at times become a full-blown Anxiety attack where it becomes unbearable and quite debilitating to carry on normal functioning. Anxiety for me can lead to stress that builds up and further causes feelings of overwhelm.

2. WHAT ARE A FEW THINGS YOU WISH PEOPLE KNEW ABOUT ANXIETY?

I wish people knew that Anxiety can be quite serious and debilitating for the person who goes through it. I also wish people knew that the sometimes inexplicable feelings of stress and overwhelm can be linked to Anxiety and when professional help is sought, life can be more manageable.

3. WHAT IS IT LIKE WORKING OR BEING HIGH-FUNCTIONING WITH ANXIETY?

It really helps to know that the feelings that accompany Anxiety are temporary and they do pass. I have learnt to recognise triggers and practice distress tolerance and self-soothing skills (like cold water splashes, rhythmic breathing exercises, writing down thoughts, taking a quick walk) that get me through difficult times.

I also try to stick to a routine and have a regular meditation practice which has significantly reduced Anxiety attacks.

Reaching out and seeking help when it feels overwhelming is something that I had to learn along the way. In terms of managing work and everyday stuff, it helps to break things into small chunks and not taking up more than I can handle (which is difficult for me). And last but not the least, learning to accept a bad day as just a bad day. I can start over and it's ok.

4. WHAT ARE SOME MYTHS AND FACTS THAT PEOPLE IN INDIA SHOULD KNOW?

Myth: Anxiety is not a real problem.
Fact: Anxiety issues are serious health issues that can have a debilitating effect on a person.

Myth: Anti-anxiety medication is the only way to treat Anxiety Disorders.
Fact: Medication does help relieve symptoms and may be necessary in some situations but there are a number of other ways to treat and manage Anxiety in the long run.

Myth: Anxiety is temporary, that eventually it will go away.
Fact: Fears associated with Anxiety Disorders and phobias don't necessarily disappear completely but with treatment they can be efficiently managed.

Myth: That there is a cure or that there is no cure for Anxiety.

Fact: There are a number of treatments available for Anxiety Disorders, including medication and psychotherapy that can help in effectively managing Anxiety in the long run. There is no magic cure that will make it go away permanently and suddenly.

Myth: People with Anxiety should avoid stressful situations.

Fact: While stress can trigger anxiety attacks, treatment helps in dealing with stressful situations by developing good coping mechanisms.

5. WHAT DO YOU WISH YOU KNEW WHEN YOU WERE YOUNGER? DO YOU HAVE ANY ADVICE FOR YOUR YOUNGER SELF?

Reach out, share and seek help. Humility is not just in giving but also in asking for what you need. You are not your feelings, thoughts and emotions but they are important too and signal a need, so pay attention. Be kind to yourself, it takes a lot of practice to take care of yourself.

LIVING WITH ANXIETY AND PANIC ATTACKS

Niharika Maggo

Born and brought up in New Delhi, Niharika is the Head of Growth at People Like Us Create (Pluc), having worked to build new verticals across technology, media and SaaS industries. She's a strong advocate for climate action and mental health. Niharika has lived with Anxiety for as long as she can remember. According to her, conversations about mental health need to be more actively empathetic and should start from our own communities.

I was on a metro ride, when I first recognised I was experiencing a panic attack. I became shaky, almost breathless and needed to crawl down, just hide my face and disappear somewhere. Thanks to a friend who was on a call with me at that time, I gained my breath back, could stand, and look over what was just happening to me.

This was the year 2016, I was 19 years old. And while anxiety had been a part of me since my childhood, as long as I can remember, this was the first time I could connect the dots and recognise that I needed help.

For a child who had been acutely aware of her parent's sacrifices for her, for someone who had been told to be the saviour for the people around her, I have always wanted to live up to these expectations, do more, and somehow justify the point of me being on the planet.

Most of my childhood went into hearing different stories from other people's perspective, narratives that they were comfortable to share. I was a child piecing together parts of my own family, making sense of the people around me. And there was one thing I just couldn't understand. How to reassure myself that I haven't failed if I can't make someone happy?

While I worked endlessly to become an over-achiever in school and college, Anxiety started to knock on my door in different ways. I started hiding away from personal conversation or friendships, any mention of my childhood or even talking about my favourite colour or food made me go into a series of anxious thoughts without any answers. It also brought forward constant spirals of overthinking, a never-ending spiral of negative self-talk. Even a rollercoaster between feeling everything and feeling nothing. **This also kept manifesting in**

physical forms like sweaty palms, sleeplessness, stress on my jaw.

I started working early, during the first year of my college itself and that transition while empowering in its own way came with a further set of insecurities. As I grew up the ladder to support startups that were being built up from scratch, gain experience in crucial industries and lead my own teams, imposter syndrome entered my life...**That feeling of just faking it, of not being up to the mark or being lost in the crowd.**

All through these years and my journey with my Anxiety, Niharika started disappearing. All I had were negative thoughts about my own self. Anxiety however became my cohabitant. It gave me a fear of ending up alone (without another human) but also made me isolate myself in my own little shell. And how long could I sustain myself in a world like that?

The year 2016, like I mentioned earlier, was a time when I could first understand what I was feeling. There's this analogy of treading in the ocean, where on some days you swim and on others you struggle to stay afloat. And that's exactly how I felt. Just on that day, it was the second case. I was almost drowning. On a metro ride, all I could see and think was that other people were watching me, whispering something about me, judging me. And that was enough to haunt my heart and lead me to anxious thoughts. My friend who was on a phone call with me, talked constantly through those minutes, asked me questions about the day, what I was doing, what I was holding, that eventually brought me out of that spiral.

This is when she also helped me in reaching out for therapy for the very first time. At first the idea seemed very distant because I was used to silences when it comes to my feelings. But thanks to the persistence of that friend and the way my therapist gave a safe space to even the silence and subsequently the scattered pieces of thoughts I had, I was able to start this process. The helpful part was that I had someone who could make me understand that therapy was a constructive process, it was almost like problem-solving through your life and situations, just with some help from a third-person.

My first aha moment was when my therapist made me write down all the things I say to myself and then say those to her. I couldn't even say one of those sentences to her, they were simply demeaning.

Have I stopped saying these things to myself since then? Not entirely. Do I hope that one day I won't feel like this? Of course. But the transformational thing is that now I recognise these thoughts. I know their patterns. I have a list of things I can use to counter them. And to be honest, it's a strange gift to be able to recognise and manage these emotional ripples. I wouldn't have imagined doing this a few years back.

Another few lessons from therapy that helped me through my personal journey included:

- Remembering to not put myself in a small box when I compare myself with the world. Our thoughts, knowledge, experience all intersect. Rather than my being small and yours being big.
- Problem solving! There are ways I can navigate my life or trauma experiences. It's not easy but it's possible. Now when I'm anxious about a situation I try to generate multiple solutions. And finally try to pick the one that works the best in terms of practicality, availability and ability.

• Writing your triumphs. This is not from therapy but this amazing woman called Rega Jha once said to me, "if yours is a mind better at tallying moments of defeat more than those of triumphs, then it's even more important to remember to list the victories. Count them. Let this determine who you measure yourself to be when your head hits the pillow at night."

• Looking up at the sky. I know it might sound like a normal thing. And also if you think of the pollution levels we live in. But on a positive note just looking up at the sky brings me calm and hope.

• Writing small notes to the 10-year-old me, who was just trying to show up and be a good person for the people she cared for.

It took me over 15 years to understand that other people have their own journeys, decisions, and at the end of the day they are humans too. Even if what you do isn't enough, it doesn't mean that you are not enough.

Today we're having more conversations about Anxiety. There are books, podcasts and so much more being done to include the lived-experiences of people. What I truly hope is that this helps more people understand:

1. **That it's not all in our head**: Would you say the same thing for a broken arm or diabetes? No, right? It's time you think about Anxiety and mental health issues like every other health issue.
2. **That Anxiety is not a sign of weakness**: I've done some of the strongest things in my life, and at a very young age, while dealing with Anxiety. I know so many people who do the same. Anxiety is different for different people, it takes a toll on a person and you cannot and should not judge these experiences.
3. **You don't need something specific to be anxious about**: First of all, you might not know a person's full story and, second of all, there doesn't have to be a tangible reason behind feeling anxious. It can happen at the most unexpected moments and in the most unexpected ways.

What I hope you can do instead is be a better ally:

1. **Educate yourself**. That's the first step before you become vocal about these issues or if you know that someone around you might be going through a mental health issue.
2. **Don't negate what other people might be feeling.** You don't necessarily have to validate all feelings, but you definitely shouldn't negate them or suddenly make it about yourself or someone else.
3. **Support and direct to the right resources.** I'll always be so thankful to that one friend who just was there and gave me the extra nudge to start therapy. You can

be that friend for someone too.

And to all the working professionals like me, showing kindness at the workplace and within your teams is so important. You know the world is a little broken, we have witnessed a pandemic. If there's one thing that can help anxious people around you it is simply human kindness. Once you do that, rally up for conversations and policies that stop the productivity guilt, make mental healthcare and time off work more accessible to all people that work with you.

As for me, when today at 3 am I sit to talk to my Anxiety, I try to say that you are not breaking me, you're just breaking me open for learning and unlearning a few things. To the little child I was, I say that you deserve to take up space. You're here for a reason. Even on days you feel there's none. So stay.

KAMNA'S MESSAGE TO READERS

Anxiety disorders affect a large segment of the population and in many small ways almost every person would have experienced anxiety at some point in time. Given this aspect, most people tend to be dismissive about the anxiety that might be a lot more disruptive to an individual's life, almost pushing them to disregard the early signs that could indicate the existence of a larger problem in the form of any number of Anxiety Disorders.

It is important that when you notice the signs of Anxiety, which are consistently present and persist despite the changes you attempt to bring in your situations as well as in how you are approaching them and the support systems you have put in place, that you not ignore them. Trust yourself to know that something is not ok and that it needs an intervention.

Yes, Anxiety Disorders or any other mental health related illness too often have numerous psychological and social factors associated with them which have resulted in the accumulated precipitation of the constellation of symptoms you do experience. So while we do take a medical approach to working on a mental health illness, where we look to correct the biological/neurotransmitter imbalances that cause an Anxiety Disorder, working with someone to also extricate and explicate those additional factors that would have contributed towards your life experiences and the development of your personality and temperament, shaping your belief system overall, is extremely critical.

If you know someone who has an Anxiety Disorder or witness someone experiencing symptoms of Anxiety in a public space, be empathetic. Instead of being a spectator and contributing to the individual's Anxiety, either provide them aid and support, or move away from the situation so that the person is not further embarrassed. This embarrassment can contribute towards a heightened experience of anxiousness and can prevent an individual from engaging in the social settings in which they experienced the Anxiety in the future.

LIVING WITH ANXIETY AND PANIC ATTACKS

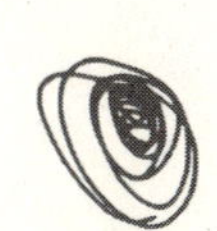

Girish Iyer

This story first appeared as a first-person story[9] *on* The Health Collective. *Girish Iyer has been working in the same organisation where he got introduced to Anxiety Disorder; and with time has realised that it's important to speak up about the struggles of mental health. He is committed to helping people with similar struggles and encourages open conversations on mental illnesses. He tweets @iamgirishiyer.*

This is a story of a 12-year-old boy who was blessed to have been born into a family with parents who encouraged him and stood as a pillar of support at every stage of life. Things were as normal as any other child of his age till the age of 11 — the usual ambitions, dreams and aspirations of anyone of that age. Until things changed completely. At the age of 12, there was a diagnosis of Depression — an illness which we don't talk about often, considering the stigma it carries in our minds.

This is my story — that 12-year-old is now 28.

As a pre-teen, I started withdrawing from everything, including giving up on studies; I ended up completely in social withdrawal, which lasted for four years. I was inside the darkest phase, with no sight of dawn, and the nights kept getting darker and darker. In India, something like this is usually considered a sign of the presence of an evil spirit, so I had to face some really unusual and awkward situations, including meeting people like babas at temples and religious places, and doing rituals they recommended. I don't blame my parents for taking me to them because they are slightly orthodox, and let's be honest, when something like this happens, the first thing society believes is that there's some black magic involved. In any event, I was fortunate enough to also get medical help at the same time. My parents were trying things from both ends.

Though I did get the medical help I really needed, it took almost four years for medication to kick in and for me to start seeing some sight of dawn. I started to feel like a normal individual but the four years had already made what felt like an irreversible dent in my life.

Imagine a 16-year-old boy facing friends of his age with whom he has completely cut off, only to realise that they are now academically four years ahead. I had to start again from where I had left off. But as they say, "What seem like bitter trials are often blessings in disguise." I was shown a more unconventional path to complete my education, graduating and doing further studies thanks to open universities.

So now at 24, I had a graduate degree and a post-graduate degree, and had already gone through possibly the darkest phase of my life. Or so I thought. The truth is, the real test of my life only began now, because I had to face people at job interviews and explain the hardest thing — the depressive phase and its impact on my life and education. It's not surprising I started to devalue myself after a couple of rejections. This is when I was introduced to an Anxiety Disorder which got triggered during a job interview for a company (which seemed like a dream job). A Panic Attack got triggered during the course of an interview. The experience was scary and not less than a horrible nightmare.

The experience became a regular phenomenon and kept continuing; I am now 28 years old and I still suffer from multiple panic attacks and bouts of depressive episodes on a daily basis. There were times in my life when the struggles were so overwhelming and difficult to cope with that I even thought of giving up on life. But I didn't. I always chose not to take that grave step and decided to go through the worst because I loved my parents more than anyone else and never wanted them to go through the pain of losing their loved child. **It took some years for me to realise what panic attacks were and to take some conscious efforts to learn some coping mechanisms to deal with the attacks. Even though the panic attacks still continue till date, the understanding about the triggers and warning signs has helped me deal with the illness in a better way.**

Note: If you or anyone you know feels desperate or talks about suicidal ideation, please reach out to a trained professional for help. You are not alone. You can find some third-party helplines at the end of the book.

After experiencing panic attack symptoms for a couple of years, I was put on different anti-anxiety medications and was taught some relaxation techniques by treating doctors, which didn't actually help...Though the doctor had used the term 'panic attack', I wasn't given any deep understanding about its symptoms or causes. I kept on blaming my own weakness, without realising it to be an actual illness.

Though I was going to work and continuing with day-to-day life, these experiences started becoming more severe, affecting my performance at work. It was during that time a doctor finally gave me some more information about anxiety disorders. It was then that I started gathering more information and insights on mental health, including Anxiety Disorders and Depression.

There were a number of articles, blog posts, podcasts, YouTube videos I went through to understand more about this situation. I also got psychological help as well and took some CBT (Cognitive Behavioural Therapy) technique training sessions and even attended some NLP (Neuro-Linguistic Programming) programmes.

But there were times when things used to get so overwhelming... I dialled up some suicide prevention helplines, and also started email conversations with them, not because I was feeling suicidal, but because I wanted to talk and get the things out. It did help.

... I want to share that all through this journey I have discovered so many positive qualities I possess. I consider myself fortunate and blessed to have been born with a great fighting spirit that has kept me alive and given me the courage to face life in spite of all the adversities. Even though I still struggle with my illness on a daily basis, I am equally optimistic and on the path of acceptance and healing in the best possible way, and I hope to make some positive impact on society in helping people with mental health see beyond the stigma and shame surrounding mental illness.

This is my story. Thank you for taking the time to go through it.

KAMNA'S MESSAGE TO READERS

People often think that mental health illnesses only impact adults. It is forgotten that children and adolescents too can be diagnosed with mental health related illnesses and Depression and Anxiety are the two most common illnesses that affect the mental health and well-being of the young. This lack of understanding is often a contributory factor towards help not being sought for the problems that might be causing the young person's grades to fall or social interactions to be affected.

It is important for us to start recognising the reality of mental health illnesses and the ways in which they can impact the lives of young people. We can have our faith and belief systems which maintain hope, but there is no substitute for treatment for mental health problems.

Just like one would treat a physical health related problem, it is important to seek intervention from an expert (a psychologist or a psychiatrist) at the earliest to ensure that the prognosis is better for a young person who is diagnosed with the illness.

Additionally, co-morbidity in mental health related illnesses is a known reality and often even though an individual may be initially diagnosed with one illness, later on the symptom profile can change and a different illness can emerge. This too is very much akin to physical health problems and like in the case of physical health ailments, seeking treatment is a must.

An early diagnosis for a young individual can be very difficult to cope with. As much as adults around them may not be aware of what might be going on, the young individual is even more uninformed about what is happening. The apprehension and lack of understanding can contribute towards increased withdrawal and isolation which can impede social relationships and academic pursuits. Further, these would overall have a strong negative influence upon the young individual's sense of self, self-esteem, confidence and worthiness.

Creating the right support mechanisms in such a scenario is extremely critical as is the need to ensure there is on-going therapeutic intervention. Working with family members to help them build their understanding of the illness, its nature and progression is a must and it is equally important to communicate with the young person's school/college to ensure that there is adequate understanding and support that is being provided in these spaces to ameliorate the impact of the illness as far as possible.

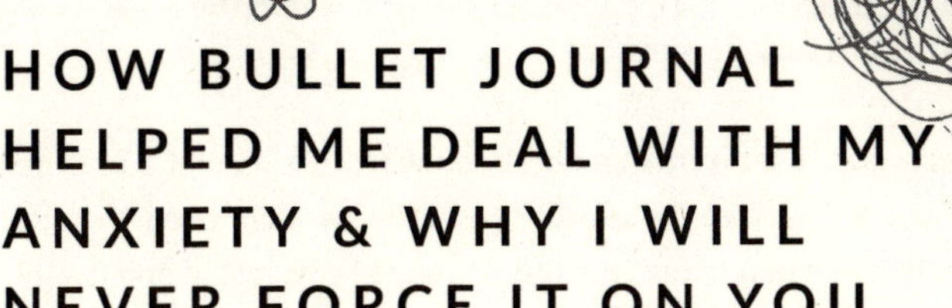

HOW BULLET JOURNAL HELPED ME DEAL WITH MY ANXIETY & WHY I WILL NEVER FORCE IT ON YOU

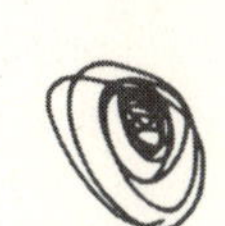

Rajashree Gandhi

Rajashree Gandhi first shared a version of this chapter in a piece[10] *for* The Health Collective. *Rajashree Gandhi is a writer, a teacher and a writing teacher, who grew up in Nagpur. Currently, she is working as a Senior Teaching Associate at the SIFF Scholars Program for under-resourced children in Bengaluru. She also writes and distributes short essays on mind, body, and more in her newsletter 'Evolving & Enough'. Find her @raju_tai on Twitter or Insta.*

Google 'bullet journaling' and you will know what a long-lasting trend it has been. The system has helped a range of people to do a variety of things, and even supported mental health survivors to cope.

Almost four years ago, I set it up in a notebook worth Rs 35 and a blue ball point pen. I had started to feel the anxiety beneath my skin, even though I couldn't name it. I had decided to quit the pits of stress I was lost in and find relief and meaning and purpose. I was starting an important journey in my life, and within a few days, this notebook system promised to be an ally. I was quite lost and directionless in almost every part of my life. I couldn't come 'home' to myself, through the traffic of Anxiety and restlessness.

Gradually I could arrive at my lifelong passion and aspiration to be a writer, a teacher and a writing teacher. I could gather some wholeness in my life. The five bullet journals on my shelf are the records of my journey. And my sixth bullet journal is still helping me tackle new challenges. It still feels like possessing an extra mind that helps me create a better ambience for the existing one.

Of course it didn't transform me into a calm warrior who's slaying at life. But it did help me identify the negative loops and patterns that hold me captive, so that I could start loosening their grip on me. It did deliver on its promise: track the past, organise the present and prepare for the future.

This essay is part enthusiastic recommendation, part mindful warning. Bullet journal gave me the tools to deal with my Anxiety. But like other trending ideas, it can also induce anxiety in some people.

A NOTE ON PRODUCTIVITY INTERNET AND MENTAL HEALTH

If you have been on the internet as long as me, you might have landed up in this particularly shiny corner of the internet, the corner of self-help and productivity. Behind the shine, there are aggressive promises and intimidating voices reducing you to a machine who can increase their 'output'. It is often insensitive to minorities, survivors of mental health issues and chronic illness. It puts the entire onus to lead happy, productive, successful lives on you, the reader, without questioning the system. It ends up increasing the very frustrations it proclaims to fight. I had never expected to find a 'solution' there.

But here's the thing, this solution, the bullet journal, changed my life, and is quite capable of failing to change yours. I share my experience here, not with any lofty claims, but only with a gentle nudge to give it a shot.

WHAT IS A BULLET JOURNAL

The bullet journal system is born with the holy union of a blank notebook and a black pen. It's not something one can rush out to buy, but has to be set up, much like how we set up our room — according to our needs.

A part of bullet journal's genius is that it was designed by Ryder Carroll inspired by his own learning disability.[11] Caroll's 2015 video on YouTube ('How to Bullet Journal') is the only reference one needs to get started with bullet journaling.

Today there's a large online community of 'bullet journalists' who exchange new ideas to build on the basic system Caroll created. Unlike their spreads which are very artsy and colourful, Caroll keeps it simple and minimalistic. While it can be soothing to add colours to the pages, not doing so is completely alright.

Having said that, maintaining even a basic bullet journal does require time. But if I compare it to the total time I have lost to being overwhelmed, lost and distracted, I'd say it's a pretty good deal!

HOW IS BULLET JOURNAL DIFFERENT FROM PLANNERS, DIARIES AND APPS?

A bullet journal can be endlessly adapted to suit oneself. It provides a gathering place to our to-do lists. It doesn't cage us like planners and dated diaries. Bullet journal gave me both: structure and flexibility.

A host of journaling and task management apps are available today. But there's something about using pen and paper that is more enabling in the process of self-management, as opposed to the flickering distractions of a screen.

JOURNALING THROUGH ANXIETY SPECIFIC BEHAVIOURS

I had this need for perfectionism ever since I was a kid. I would only scribble on the back pages of the cutesy notebooks I had collected over the years, too scared to 'spoil' them with my thoughts, some of which felt unworthy, mediocre and ugly. Ryder Carroll's system makes it difficult to leave pages for the elusive tomorrow, and pushes us to focus on the present.

Anxiety feels like a bunch of voices speaking in loud volume at the same

time. Writing my thoughts, tasks, goals, aspirations into the daily, monthly and future logs of the bullet journal helped me slow down the trains of my thought. Everything else from workshop ideas to how-to-cope-with-winter got logged in 'Collections'.

Obvious acts like taking a bath and taking medicines may be easy for many, but mental health issues often cause you to forget basic tasks. Outsourcing the mental load to checklists and trackers frees up abundant space for creativity.

Anxiety has also been constant self-doubt, guilt, confusion wherein I blew up every little instance of failure and downplay my achievements. Coupling to-do lists with 'done' lists, as suggested by a bullet-journalist, helped me understand how I spend my time, and the umpteen things I do get done without knowing it.

'HOW WE SPEND OUR DAYS IS HOW WE SPEND OUR LIVES'

Writer Annie Dillard had said, how we spend our days is how we spend our lives. Unlike other planners, bullet journal allowed me to record my efforts outside professional commitments. I realised how life is made richer by making gestures for our loved ones, creatively articulating our politics, as well as cooking, cleaning, self-soothing. Failures at work could no longer define my entire worth, as I had a full, top view of my life through my journal. I wrote wish-lists to remember what I want to cook or read, notes to remember what I need to share with my therapist, and habit trackers to form new habits.

Bullet journal helped me unplug from the world and connect to myself, considering one voice at a time. It sculpted parts of my loneliness into solitude. Most importantly, it helped me to speak to myself with trust. For people like me who are interested in living an unscripted, unconventional life, such tools ensure we live intentionally.

BEYOND THE FEAR OF QUITTING OR BEING JUDGED

Seeing the hype around bullet journals can be triggering for people with Anxiety. Another pit one might fall into is that of perfectionism and compulsive maintenance of the journal. It is tempting to indulge in comparison and perfectionism while maintaining a bullet journal, but it is honesty, playfulness and curiosity that lead towards the juicier, deeper, satisfying kind of journaling.

Bullet journal was an aide for my anxious mind and not a revolutionary lifestyle to be showcased online. Perhaps, that is why it continues to feel special and intimate. It fills me with hope to imagine people who struggle with their mind, finding their own special, intimate systems and solutions.

KAMNA'S MESSAGE TO READERS

Working through your Anxiety and finding the means and mechanism to do so is an important step. Much of this process is a process of discovery, as there is no one-size-fits-all solution that can be put into place.

This process can also be difficult for individuals as the Anxiety in itself can be rather debilitating and facing lack of success in being able to manage can be rather difficult and inadvertently lead to an increase in anxiety as one can begin to feel as though solutions aren't working. Maintaining a sense of balance during these times is imperative as is being willing to continue the process of exploration as you move forward to manage your Anxiety.

Often people can make strong recommendations about the veracity of a particular approach. It is important that even as you try it, you maintain an openness to the knowledge that it might not necessarily work for you. This would allow you to be able to manage the disappointment you are likely to feel which can otherwise become unmanageable.

Even as you explore techniques, if you feel you are struggling to determine the best approach for yourself, do not hesitate to reach out to an expert who can work with you on the same. The support of another can be helpful in this regard as it would allow for the balancing out of the negative thought process that can easily develop in such scenarios.

NOT
ALONE

CREATIVE LICENCE | IN HER OWN WORDS

Ilina Acharya

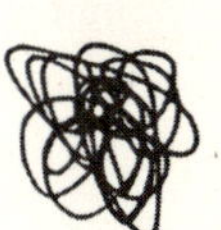

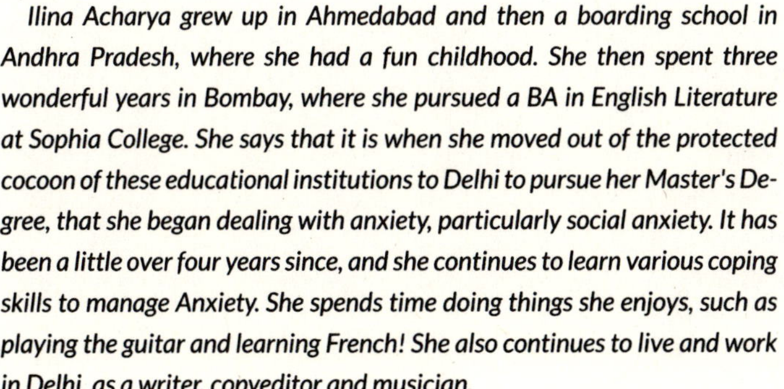

Ilina Acharya grew up in Ahmedabad and then a boarding school in Andhra Pradesh, where she had a fun childhood. She then spent three wonderful years in Bombay, where she pursued a BA in English Literature at Sophia College. She says that it is when she moved out of the protected cocoon of these educational institutions to Delhi to pursue her Master's Degree, that she began dealing with anxiety, particularly social anxiety. It has been a little over four years since, and she continues to learn various coping skills to manage Anxiety. She spends time doing things she enjoys, such as playing the guitar and learning French! She also continues to live and work in Delhi, as a writer, copyeditor and musician.

IN HER OWN WORDS: NOTE TO READER

On August 5, 2019, the Indian government abrogated Article 370 and in one fell swoop did away with Kashmir's special status. On the day of the news, I felt a pit of anxiety in my stomach. My anxiety found its expression in this nazm; in trying to describe the situation in Kashmir, I ended up inscribing my deeply personal experience with anxiety. I would like to share that with you.

Mental illness is extremely difficult to explain or describe. Art, music and literature, is one of those open spaces where I find possibility opening up through symbols, analogy and metaphor. I hope this poem does that for you.

☺ ☺ ☺

Untitled

Time moves on
Day follows another
Setting sun
casts a bloody hue
upon the sky
Who knows
what time will tell?
Just a faint disquiet
heard amidst heart's chaos
Go ask the setting sun
what will tomorrow be?
We sit in anticipation
nurturing grief

The business of living
has left us tired
Here death
is a familiar face

Go ask the bare streets
how long they can bare
Here we have learnt to
recognize their quiet grief
Deeper than silence
call of heart's ocean
Which way to go?
No map will show
Breath turns
to breathlessness
We will pave the road ahead
in waiting

☺☺☺

Original Nazm in Urdu

waqt guzarta gaya
din guzarte gaye
khoon ki chingariyon mein
sooraj dhalta gaya
kaun kahe
waqt ko kya pata

bas ek aahat si
aur dil mein ek shor sa
dhalte sooraj se tum puchho
kal kya dikhlaaoge?
tham kar behthe hai hum
ghamon ko pal rahen hai sabhi

duniya ki duniyadari se
tang aa chuke
maut ke chehre se
bhi vaaqif hum hai yahaan
sheher ke sadkon se tum puccho
aur kitna seh paaoge?
tumhari chuppi ki chhupi niraashi
pahchaane hai hum sabhi
sannate se bhi chup hai
dariya-e-dil ki pukar
kis taraf hai jaana
koi naqsha bhi na jaane
dum ghutkar
ghut chuka hai
raah dekhkar banaaenge
hum raasta

CREATIVE LICENCE | THE ANXIOUS HAT

Jessica Xalxo

This story[12] *first appeared in* The Health Collective. *Jessica Xalxo is a creative strategist, writer and independent journalist based in Mumbai, India. A strategic firebrand, Xalxo works with Grammy and Oscar-winning artists, celebrated poets and game-changing digital creators at A&R agency SIGN India, innovating and ideating to push the ante on how the world experiences art. She has previously helmed the role of Staff Writer at* Rolling Stone *India, where she built the iconic publication's native film and television vertical. Xalxo is also the author of the Red Elephant Foundation's* Speaking Our Truth: A Curriculum on Non-Violent Communication, *a book based on renowned psychologist Dr Marshall B. Rosenberg's pathbreaking peace-building process.*

IN HER OWN WORDS: NOTE TO READER

'The Anxious Hat' is a fictionalised narrative based on personal experience. I wrote this short story to share my experience with Anxiety; to translate what it's like to repeatedly question one's every thought and action, to dread and be unnerved by the unknown. I've lived with Anxiety since adolescence, writing this story just before reaching out for professional aid in my late teenage years. **Anxiety is now a constant companion; neither friend nor foe.**

☺☺☺

There had been a moment that morning. Just one.

A single ray of sunshine had pierced the otherwise outwardly aesthetic room. Almost shooting at my head, its golden tendril reflected off of the walls, before losing its novelty and direction. A single yellow spot amidst the black and white of my living squarespace.

It was there. I had felt it. Basked in it even. Hah!

And then like a thought unchased, with no heed for a request, it was gone. Just like the person who ghosts on you.

It had been courteous enough to leave a replacement. A substitute in abundance. For it had left not just one thought but a myriad coiling sentences, nestled in my head, latching themselves on to the crook of my brain. In the mellow afternoon light, it had placed in the once haloed spot a hat.

What a common yet largely unused accessory — even in the tropical weather of the city — and oft, unspoken of too.

Had it known it was going to be draughty outside? Perchance. That wouldn't be a wild guess, given the temperament of the weather lately. But it did not know me well. I did not wear hats, and this one? It did not sit well.

It was a black hat, a fedora, I think. Its felt encompassed most of the top of my head and half of my ears, so that when I put it on, the thrum of the world ceased at once. The only voice I heard was my own. My own words, my own thoughts, my own fantasies, my own reassurances and my own validations. And as my hair rose to meet the hat's roof, as if joining with the fabric, my head accepted this gift like it had no choice. But really, it did. It, no, I always did. Didn't I? Alas, meeting the fate of most good thoughts, my mind shied away from tracing this one to its very end.

It was a safe space, really. The fedora. A singular pocket of existence, with as many avenues of imagination as the hair follicles on my young flaking scalp. If I could store all my thoughts in this hat, especially those that corresponded with its colour, these thoughts, would they be contained? I might not even have to speak them. No soul would ever know the expanses, the tall worlds my mind built with predictions of the speech and movements of the world, not always true but all too real to me.

What relief, I chimed to myself. But what kind of justice would that be, really? A shaky resounding laugh escaped me, taking several breaths with it. The sighs slowly failed as they tried to keep up with my mind and the conclusions it was arriving at. There would still be the comprehending to do. Thoughts and thinking held each other by the hand. And that was where all the trouble lay after all. At least, this way, no one else would know. This could be my safe space.

And thus, I became one with the fedora. These were my thoughts after all. Contained. Within me. ***How destructive would they be?***

The hat was boundlessly snug. I could close my eyes and never leave the seemingly infinite folds in its abyss of darkness. So many velvet corners of granite coolness to settle into and be lost in — forever. All sights and smells beyond reach and amiss here in this dream of night. Oh no, waking would be unbearable. The thought of raising the shutters and my body off the bed — that might have been where the misery lay after all.

And then, I heard it. The hat. *It was speaking!*

There was a small congregation forming within the hat. Voices! All mine. Murmuring at first, then slowly gaining in octave, and rising, to a lilting cacophony of screams, as they curled, in smoky wisps, around my heart.

THERE IS SO MUCH TO BE DONE. SO MUCH. TOO MUCH.
ALL THINGS THAT I DON'T WANT TO DO WITH A FEW EXCEPTIONS.
ALWAYS A FEW. SOMETIMES TOO LITTLE TO MATTER.
TO BE DONE, MUCH THE SAME.
I WON'T FINISH DOING THEM.

In that moment, I realised I was Atlas. There would never be an escape for me. The hat could only be my requiem, not repose.

Breathe, I reminded myself. *Think of something else. Anything else. Try and come up with a new thought to replace every old cycle of notion. Engage your mind with mint ideas. Think. Jump. Again and again.* Anything could be better than this. This did work, it always did. For a few spells of time. Until it didn't. And then the hat's call was too potent not to heed.

The tasks of the day seemed insurmountable. Nevertheless, I would do them. And sincerely so. I always tried, didn't I? What good was that in a globe of millions of intentions and actions — I did not know. But what if I couldn't? What if I couldn't complete my tasks? I would fail and then there would be too much and too many to lose. More than I could bear.

Will she still talk to me if I don't submit my part of the Gender Project on time?

I'm way behind on my writing projects and she probably sees it as a lack of commitment.

Why can't I work at a normal pace like the others? My ass will be fired soon.

I am going to die alone and if I don't work before then, I will die alone and broke.

Am I even worthy of realising my dream?

Is my dream even for me?

The whole team is going to realise I'm a sham sooner or later.

I take too long to get a simple task done.

Sincerity is not the same as results.

Maybe it is that most tasks don't interest me. No, that's definitely it.

But some things must be done anyway.

Get yourself together, you've always had a healthy if not crazy work ethic.

It's work or the void, you have a choice.

Occupy a space.

There are those exams that need to be given too. Correction : re-exams.

Everybody's going to give up on me.

I don't know if I can do this.

I am too scared to find out.

Oh, Lucia also requested me to set up a blog page for her tourism business.

I have to call up Aunt Priscilla.

When was the last time I caught up with Tasneem? She must hate me now.

I am overly saturated in one field.

Dad thinks working from home isn't work.

I am too dead to want a social life.

I am definitely going to be fired tomorrow.

My parents are getting older and nearing retirement. I need to step up more.

YOU COMPLETELY FORGOT ABOUT PRIORITISING COLLEGE ONCE AGAIN!

I took off the hat as I felt the voices forming a vice-like grip around my throat, clenching my scream. The voices would subdue me. Unless... unless, I did something.

Quick! Jumping from the bed and onto the creamy marble floor, I fumbled to find my slippers and made my way to the white desk that sat beside the bedroom window. I dipped my hand into the pen stand, telling myself to ignore the sheath of dust on the pen I had selected. They were all the same anyway. Where was the time to dust when there was so much to be done? I would probably be found smothered by a dust bunny if and when I lived alone. That is if I ever lived to save up enough to move out.

Focus! I screamed at myself. There's work to be done.

I laid the voices of the hat out and onto paper. To write them. Quantify them. Give them basis and ground. I had found work to be a saviour back when the thoughts had gotten bad. It had helped me rewire and adjust to the new normal. But the thoughts never ever did leave me. Not for too long.

I translated the voices into 8 tasks for my to-do list. Okay, 8-and-a-half. Some were filler tasks – though I treated them all the same. Each task would take some time of their own, but each was do-able. I could do them. I would do them. And I would make it through.

After all, I had even taken off the hat. Acknowledged its existence. Parted with it. Or at least, I had tried. Now, it was only up to my mind to contain the thoughts. No escape or considerations of a final void. Recovery was better than requiem. Maybe.

I turned to look at the bed, wanting, no needing so badly to wrap myself in the comforting shroud of my bedsheet.

'Just brush your teeth and eat your breakfast,' I said aloud. Speaking to myself again. I only ever spoke multiple authoritative sentences to myself anymore, in stark contrast to my outwardly social and pliant self.

Put one foot in front of the other. A smile when in doubt. A call should you collapse, but maybe not. What if nobody answers? Those who tell you to call when you need them are being courteous. Don't actually take them up on the offer. How could they possibly help you? You'll lose the people you have if they learn of the real you. Just be where you're most comfortable and not bothersome. But still, try to push the ante — you've to get somewhere in life and you could start with getting out of this. This doesn't have to be your every day reality. But it is, isn't it? Will every day be like this? It will.

Mom would hate me when she realised that I hadn't been able to get myself to go to college. Again. I couldn't. How could I tell her that? Maybe once the early morning stopped feeling like a second vacuum and college another concrete social obligation of sharing space, I'll want to go. I'll have to want to go. Tomorrow, I will. Please, please do, I beg myself, crying mutedly as I shuffled, taking questioned steps, to the bathroom.

"We could seek professional help, you know?" I heard one last whisper from the hat as it sat, taunting and perched upon my space.

'Oh honey, nobody believes that you are real, and nobody will believe me about you.'

Nobody.

Till date, I live varied renditions of the hour on repeat.

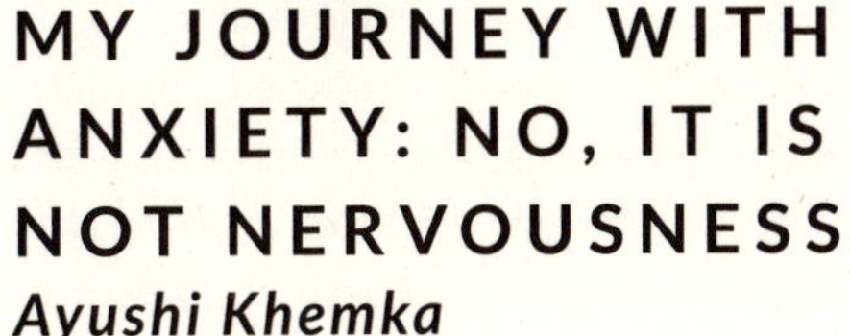
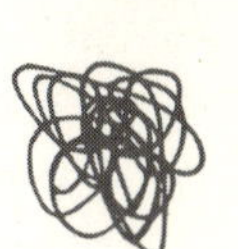

MY JOURNEY WITH ANXIETY: NO, IT IS NOT NERVOUSNESS

Ayushi Khemka

This piece[13] *earlier appeared in* The Health Collective. *A 27-year-old Delhi girl, Ayushi Khemka, created Mental Health Talks India in April 2018. Living with depression and anxiety herself, she wishes to end the stigma around mental health in India. She is also a PhD scholar working on the intersections of gendered violence and social media. She believes in channelising one's vulnerabilities into an honest conversation that can potentially bring about a change in how we live and exist in the world.*

A year or two ago, I remember seeing a popular 'women-centric digital platform in India' selling their own merchandise, specifically a hoodie with 'ANXIETY! ANXIETY! ANXIETY!' written over it in big, bold letters and bright colours. On probing further, I found that the product description contained words like 'quirky' to flesh out the mood of the product. While capitalism does keep on disappointing me every now and then, this niche product marketed at young girls like myself, treating 'anxiety' like a fun, little quirk with a set aesthetic jarred me to no extent. I have been battling Anxiety for around three years now, or at least I am aware that I have Anxiety for three years. As someone whose day job as a researcher requires her to examine all things social media, I could gauge where the brand was coming from. It was coming from the place where mental health is becoming a hot cake that everyone wants a piece of. It is, to put it simply, becoming a buzzword for marketing agencies across sectors. Despite knowing all this, it did hurt me intensely, seeing that something for which I have been taking pills, seeing a therapist every week, spending a lot of money to treat and manage, was described in a frivolous way as a quirk.

My struggle with Anxiety began alongside my struggle with Depression. **Now, I had heard about how Depression and Anxiety are those two pesky extended relatives in your family, who always come uninvited to your place, you don't like them, they don't like you and nor do they like each other. And when all three of you come together, you can only expect chaos.**

However, experiencing all of this first-hand was quite a confusing experience, to begin with. To give a little context, my struggles with mental health began during my higher studies while I was pursuing a research degree. Being a 23-year-old student, a lot of my anxieties were around the coursework, my academic performance, the academic stress passed off as rigour in our educational

institutions and the like. Clearly, due to my depression, I was unable to focus on my studies and was quite disinterested in the course. However, with my Anxiety, I was also obsessing over the coursework and my disability to gauge the nuances of it. This dichotomous mode of being is what troubled me then and continues to bother me even today after almost three years have passed.

Living with Anxiety is extremely difficult to explain. **More so, in the current social media ethos, when anxiety (along with other forms of mental health issues) has been reduced to an aesthetic and a quirk to bedazzle one's personality or lack thereof**. Anxiety is not nervousness. Yes, every single one of us feels nervous at some point in our lives but all of us do not take medication for or seek treatment for anxiety as a disorder, as something that starts affecting your day-to-day routine and makes you a jittery mess. Finding anxiety translated into some cute and even intellectual trait in the annals of Instagram has been a source of anxiety for me. I wonder if this is ironic, but who's to say. As a person who lives with Anxiety, I find a lot of the things that are quite normative and normal for others, extremely difficult to navigate through. Loud noises increase my heartbeat so much that I can't hear the noises after some point. Crowded places make me feel as if the world is closing in on me. A basic, generic fight with my loved ones makes me feel like this is the end of the world for me. On some days, merely after waking up it feels like a thousand elephants are trampling upon my chest. A slight change in my schedule or a minor hiccup in my work makes me run to the loo a number of times that I still don't feel comfortable disclosing on a public platform. I wish at least one of these things were 'cute' or 'aesthetic' but alas, that is never the case.

Anxiety is disabling in ways that a lot of people can't even begin to imagine. I remember my first ever concrete verbalisation of suicidal thoughts occurred

whilst I was having an anxiety attack. To tell you the sheer absurdity of Anxiety and the overpowering characteristic of it, let me tell you that the first time I wished to kill myself was because I was unable to perform at a family function because I was not is a position to do that. That is all it took for my brain to convince me to end my life and be gone for good. Of course, there was a lot of backstory attached to the incident and the location, but my anxiety needed just one minute change in my schedule for the next 30 minutes to tell me that I needed to die. As I type this, I am still baffled by the magnanimity and disabling nature of Anxiety. To be truly honest, it still does not fully make sense to me.

There are numerous incidents that have happened since then, some everyday incidents and some exceptional ones, all of which have made me feel incapacitated within myself. While medicines have helped me to a great extent, taking therapy and having a tiny but reliable care network have done wonders. As repetitive and borderline cliché as it may sound, but talking does help. Knowing that you can lay bare your vulnerabilities in front of your loved ones and then not be judged or chided for it is a cathartic feeling, so much so that even while typing this, I'm heaving a sigh of relief.

However, these realisations came only quite late in my journey with Anxiety. I'd kill to go back into time and just let it be known to my younger self that Anxiety is a real issue and not something that I am making up on my own. The world might continue to call me a drama queen because it does not know how to handle the very concept of an 'extra' woman, let alone an anxious extra woman. I do believe that had I paid more attention to listening to the needs of my mind and body and less on how people would perceive me, I would have been in a much better place a lot earlier. I would also remind myself that Anxiety is going to affect my body too with horrible back pains and permanently tense shoulder muscles and that I better listen to my psychiatrist and get down to doing some exercise.

As is with the physical manifestations of Anxiety, it does get extremely tiring hearing the nagging voice in my head over and over again asking me to recheck if the word I just spelt is right or not, if the post I just read had that exact word that I think I read or not, if people like me or not. The list is endless. What the list is not is a fancy way of describing nervousness. It is not something that goes away instantaneously if one asks me to 'calm down'. **It is a tear-inducing, panic-striking, body-trembling, mind-numbing condition that has nothing to do with the pastel coloured aesthetics that multiple brands and influencers of today's social media world would like to suggest.**

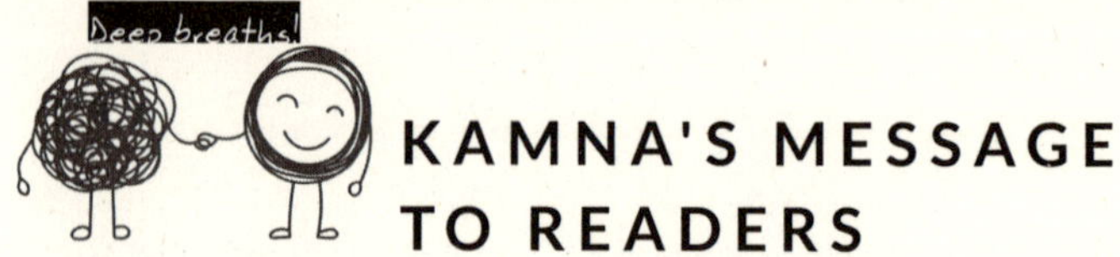

KAMNA'S MESSAGE TO READERS

The experience of having an Anxiety Disorder is unique to every individual. Yes, there are specific signs and symptoms and criteria that must be met in order to reach a diagnosis of the illness. However, the way it affects an individual to alter and shape their life is unique to every person.

As a result, the treatment process too needs to be tailor-made to every individual. This is more specifically the case when we consider therapeutic interventions for those who are diagnosed with the illness. It is essential that one recognise this aspect to be able to understand that the journey through a mental health problem like an Anxiety DIsorder thus may be varied for different people and comparisons don't help.

The end goal is to reach a point where the individual is able to manage their Anxiety, live a wholesome life, work, be productive and function effectively in their relationships while taking care of their own selves. Towards this end, the treatment process forms a critical element and it is crucial that you identify the right experts to work with. Concurrently, ensure you have the right support systems in place and that people around you too are informed about what Anxiety is and how it affects your life.

This too is a process and can be a rather arduous one for any person but nevertheless one that we must undertake to be able to take care of yourself as you work through the illness. It can involve many pitfalls, including having to make difficult choices for yourself, with your work and even your relationships. As a result, working with a therapist can be rather beneficial, as a therapist can support you through this journey and help you stay centred, grounded and balanced as you work through things.

PART TWO

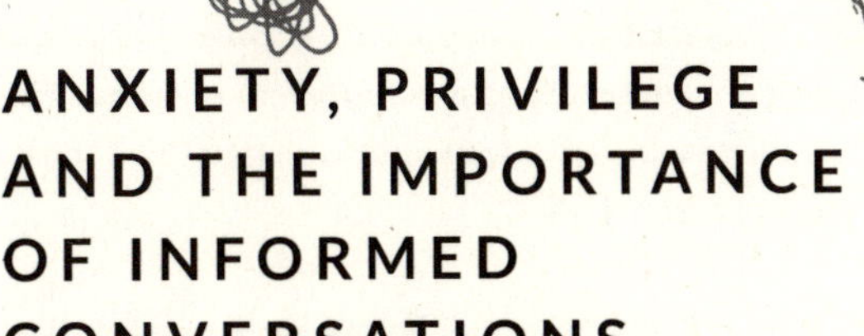

ANXIETY, PRIVILEGE AND THE IMPORTANCE OF INFORMED CONVERSATIONS

An Interview with Tanmoy Goswami

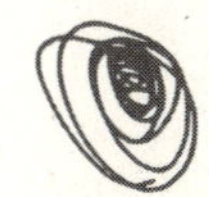

Tanmoy Goswami is a Delhi-based journalist, formerly with The Correspondent, *probably the first and possibly the only 'Sanity Correspondent' in the world. He is the author of the 'Sanity by Tanmoy' newsletter and writes on the politics, economics and culture of mental health, driven by his lifelong personal tryst with Depression and Anxiety. Earlier, Tanmoy was associate editor at ET Prime. He is a winner of IE Business School, Madrid's Asian Journalism Prize. He spends much of his personal time on suicide prevention advocacy and improving media literacy on mental health issues. Tanmoy grew up in the industrial town of Durgapur in West Bengal and has lived all across India, but you're most likely to find him on Twitter, where he goes by @toymango.*

AMRITA: This pandemic year we are seeing more conversations around Mental Health than ever. Do you feel that you've seen an uptick in people talking about Anxiety as well as Depression? And crucially, are we able to navigate folks to the help they might need, in India?

TANMOY: Anecdotally, there definitely does seem to be a surge in symptoms, though one can't be sure if that's true clinically in the absence of data. There has hardly been a day in the past several weeks that I haven't had at least one person reach out to me asking for help for themselves or their family or friends. Elderly people in my own family have been going through severe crises. And as the father of a two-and-a-half-year-old, I'm increasingly troubled by what I am reading and hearing about the pandemic and the lockdown's psychological impact on young children — a demographic we don't talk about at all in the adult business of mental health.

I've myself been struggling with a peculiar phenomenon that I call '4 o'clock Anxiety', like the 4 o'clock rainfall in equatorial regions. I get a huge burst of panic at that time almost every day, which only relents once I pop an SoS pill. My therapist helped me understand that this pattern could be the result of pent-up anxiety about productivity. As another day nears its end, my mood dips because I worry that I once again failed to finish all the things on my to-do list. Apparently, a lot of people are experiencing this obnoxious feeling.

Obviously, everyone has different triggers, and not all the stories I am familiar with can be directly attributed to the pandemic. But it does seem like a watershed, in that it has given a decisive push to mental health awareness — at least in a section of the privileged circles. Clearly, as with so many other social and structural problems, the pandemic has blown the cover off the cesspit of distress that we've been sitting on.

That leads me to the second part of your question, about access to help. As a journalist and user/survivor, I am able to connect some people with reliable professionals, especially in the bigger cities and towns. But the stark reality of India, which we keep repeating ad nauseam, is that we don't have nearly enough of these professionals going around — and probably never will.

This entire period has strengthened two of my core beliefs:

1. Awareness without access to care is cruel.
2. India needs community-based mental health interventions focused on prevention rather than cure. Rather than DMing strangers on Twitter, people should be able to find support in their own communities and neighbourhoods. I am thinking of the Atmiyata project in the villages of Maharashtra and Pune, where school dropouts are helping neighbours manage emotional problems before they turn malignant. Or the Friendship Bench in Zimbabwe — a country that reportedly has fewer than 20 psychiatrists for the entire population and which doesn't even have a local-language equivalent of 'depression' — where grandmothers trained to listen have helped thousands of people in pain. Both Atmiyata and the Friendship Bench have passed scientific scrutiny. They offer a framework for the kind of sustainable 'help' that we all deserve.

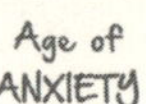

AMRITA: Would you say we are living in an Age of Anxiety? How important is it to understand how to manage the disorder?

TANMOY: To answer this question, we have to go back a little — to the history of human evolution! In evolutionary terms, anxiety was an adaptive emotion. It protected early humans from unseen threats. Anxiety told them to run when there was a rustling in the bushes because it could be a hungry lion. French psychiatrist Marc-Antoine Crocq[14] writes that Greek and Latin physicians and philosophers identified anxiety as a medical disorder, but it was not classified as a separate illness between classical antiquity and the late 19th century. The German psychiatrist Emil Kraepelin (1856–1926) mainstreamed the study of severe Anxiety in manic depression, and then gradually Anxiety burgeoned as a diagnostic category.

American psychologist Graham L. Davey also talks about 'a gradual shift in the social ethos surrounding anxiety.[15] This change has been almost contradictory in the messages it sends to us. We're told anxiety is a legitimate response to the stresses of modern living, and anxiety is almost considered a status symbol that signals how busy and successful we are. But, in the same breath, we're led to believe that anxiety is a problem that needs treatment.'

Today, Anxiety is the most common psychological disorder in the US, and some say anti-anxiety medication are a grav-

er source of addictions than opioids. According to a CNBC report,[16] overdose deaths involving popular drugs such as Xanax, Librium, Valium and Ativan, commonly used to treat Anxiety, phobias, panic attacks, seizures and insomnia, quadrupled between 2002 and 2015. In 2015, benzo overdoses accounted for 8,791 deaths, up from 1,135 in 1999. I explored all this in detail in an article for *The Correspondent*.[17]

But as I also argued in the same article, I think our relationship with Anxiety is broken. If only we were a little more anxious as a species in the early days of the pandemic and had not partied with abandon in Miami or Berlin or hosted football matches in Italy despite signs of clear and present danger, we may have lost fewer lives. While paying attention to anxiety was once second nature, what we now glorify is just the opposite: rebelling against it and undermining it in a dangerous display of bravado. From climate change to the coronavirus, this line of thinking has repeatedly pushed us to act in dangerous ways, shutting out those who know better as 'conspiracy theorists'. Those who are able to resist this impulse and err on the side of caution, even if it appears like an overreaction — like the South Korean government did with its relentless Covid testing strategy — are best placed to survive and make it through to the next phase of evolution, whatever that might look like.

AMRITA: Can you share some of your journey with us? In dealing with Depression and Anxiety, and talking (and tweeting in that epic thread)[18]... When did you first learn about these as a diagnosis? What were your thoughts?

TANMOY: As a diagnosis, Anxiety (and Depression) probably entered my life about 15–16 years ago, when I was in college. My reaction? I thought the therapist was trying to say I was going 'mad', and I never went back there!

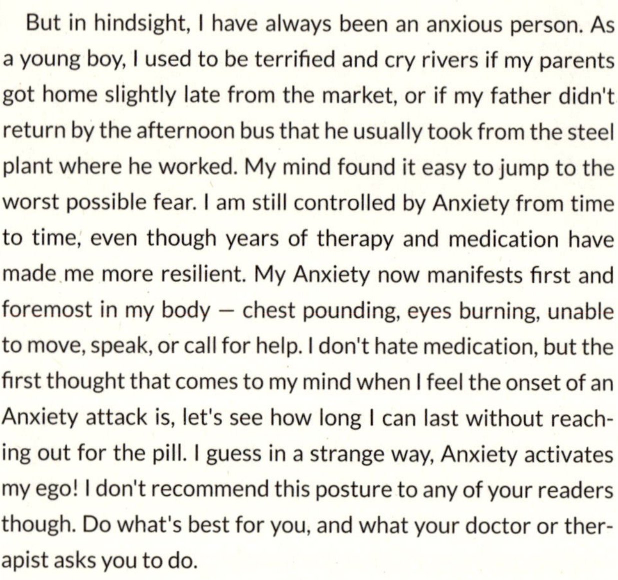

But in hindsight, I have always been an anxious person. As a young boy, I used to be terrified and cry rivers if my parents got home slightly late from the market, or if my father didn't return by the afternoon bus that he usually took from the steel plant where he worked. My mind found it easy to jump to the worst possible fear. I am still controlled by Anxiety from time to time, even though years of therapy and medication have made me more resilient. My Anxiety now manifests first and foremost in my body — chest pounding, eyes burning, unable to move, speak, or call for help. I don't hate medication, but the first thought that comes to my mind when I feel the onset of an Anxiety attack is, let's see how long I can last without reaching out for the pill. I guess in a strange way, Anxiety activates my ego! I don't recommend this posture to any of your readers though. Do what's best for you, and what your doctor or therapist asks you to do.

I know now that Anxiety runs on my mother's side (and I say this without meaning to blame anyone for passing it on to me). Growing up, I'd routinely see my grandmother and my mother (a retired nurse herself) display a lot of the 'over-worrying', 'over-thinking', 'hyperventilating' behaviour that I can now see in myself.

I remember on 9/11, my mother called me up in the college hostel sounding frightened and told me to sleep with my windows shut. I yelled at her for being absurd. Back then, no one called it Anxiety or offered to help these women. Our standard

response to people living with chronic Anxiety was — and still is to a large extent — mockery and ridicule. We patronise and infantilise them. Anxiety festers in dark places. It feeds on shame. We need to meet it with light and air. Instead, our impatience and dismissiveness makes people with Anxiety clam up even more.

AMRITA: What has helped you cope?

TANMOY: I am privileged enough to be able to talk openly about my condition — it's part of my job as a mental health journalist! — and I make full use of it. I try to defang Anxiety by constructing a narrative in which my tendency to make a mountain out of a molehill isn't a disease — it is my superpower, my window to an alternate reality that others don't have access to. To be sure, I am not trying to romanticise Anxiety, only sharing my defence mechanism. Then, of course, there is therapy and medication, which have helped me remain functional, and a safety net of family and friends — such as yourself — who keep reminding me that life isn't as bad as I suspect it is :).

AMRITA: There is an increasing effort to center the discourse, moving away from just the individual to the systemic — any thoughts here you would like to share, with the lens of 'Anxiety' as a disorder?

TANMOY: What makes us anxious? Some neurons misfiring? Some chemicals poisoning our bloodstream? Or financial insecurity? Debt? Peer pressure? Domestic violence? Insensitive bosses? Intolerance, bigotry and the creeping feeling that something in the world that we knew and loved has gone forever? I think the answer to your question lies in all these questions.

AMRITA: Your message to any reader who is concerned about Mental Health and Mental Illness in India and doesn't know quite what to do to help people?

TANMOY: Don't presume. Ask.

Don't venture advice. Listen.

Don't watch TV to educate yourself on mental health. Read *The Health Collective* and *Sanity by Tanmoy*. Don't jump into saviour mode. Put on your own oxygen mask before helping others. Finally, don't doubt your ability to help, even if you don't have a professional qualification. Wanting to help people is the only qualification you need, the rest you will learn.

AMRITA: We seem to be more comfortable talking about Anxiety and Depression in everyday conversations; but does that mean people have begun to understand what having a mental health disorder or diagnosable condition like Anxiety or Depression means? Your thoughts on this basis your experiences and maybe across languages?

TANMOY: Like I said in the first answer, I think there's been some progress in a section of the privileged circles. But we have a very, very long way to go.

As just one example, senior psychiatrists keep telling me that far too many young people in this country, even in big cities, still can't talk to their parents about their mental struggles. When they muster the courage to, they are admonished by their fam-

ilies and discouraged from seeking professional help. Also, the clinical gravity that 'depression' or 'anxiety' carries in English isn't quite there in '*tanaav*' in Hindi or '*utkantha*' in Bengali. There isn't an accessible enough conversation on these ideas in many of our languages.

But social media is helping change some of this. What we are seeing on Twitter or Instagram is a ground-up movement to democratise and distribute the mental health conversation, led purely by people with lived experience. From YouTube videos to memes on Facebook, people are expressing themselves in a million creative ways, by passing the language obstacle.

AMRITA: A few myths you would like to dispel about Anxiety in India?

TANMOY:

Myth Number 1: That Anxiety is a sign of weakness, and that everyone living with Anxiety is an 'unproductive burden' on society.

Myth Number 2: That people with Anxiety somehow enjoy being anxious and getting attention and don't want to change.

Myth Number 3: That it can't happen to you.

AMRITA: Finally, what would your message be to a younger Tanmoy?

TANMOY: Go back to the therapist, you fool!

ANXIETY, FRIENDSHIP, FAMILY AND COPING

An Interview with Pragya Tiwari

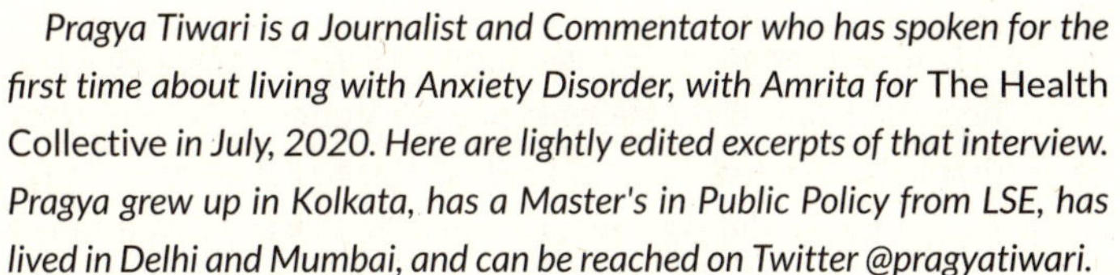

Pragya Tiwari is a Journalist and Commentator who has spoken for the first time about living with Anxiety Disorder, with Amrita for The Health Collective *in July, 2020. Here are lightly edited excerpts of that interview. Pragya grew up in Kolkata, has a Master's in Public Policy from LSE, has lived in Delhi and Mumbai, and can be reached on Twitter @pragyatiwari.*

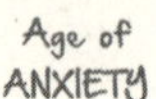

AMRITA: Can you help me contextualise this conversation because I just discovered this is the first time you're actually going to be talking about having Anxiety, or learning that you had Anxiety, and what that means.

PRAGYA: Yes, I mean we all live public lives in the sense about being vocal about issues on Twitter, taking on the government or whether it's on Instagram talking about our escapades, our parties, drinking, all of the things that were perhaps socially or morally taboo for women decades ago, or even today in certain parts of the world or certain parts of the country.

One just assumes that women like myself who have a fair degree of financial independence, education, privilege, class privilege, caste privilege, etc. will be able to get away with saying anything. And even so, like you said, this is the first time I am speaking about this to anybody outside of my absolute immediate circle of friends and family, and when I say absolute immediate, I mean really, really only a handful of people who are really really close to me have been privy to the conversation I'm about to have and the kinds of things that I had to ask myself before I decided to speak about it with you, was, well, it really mattered that I was speaking with you and it was for this forum, so that really matters.

But beyond that, I did have to ask myself the question, can this, well, this become my digital footprint? And the internet is where we live now, and somebody who googles me will come

across this, and there is this kind of anxiety, not in a clinical sense, that a prospective employer might Google this and this might be used against me, or it might be grounds, maybe not very vocally, but subconsciously (or even consciously) for discrimination, and then of course as a journalist, I write about a lot of things that can be considered provocative in many ways, and you wonder if your sanity is going to be questioned because just the foreground, any kinds of mental illness, is so intense that people just tend to conflate everything… and then of course as a woman, you're always considered hysterical.

I mean, the first mental illness that was really widely and publicly talked about was hysteria and only women were supposed to really have it, and while people don't say that out loud anymore, I don't think those kind of biases have gone away from people and society. So you worry about these things and they're very valid concerns. At the end of the day, we are women who have fought against all kinds of odds, this is not discounting my privilege, of course there are women who have it much harder, but we have fought and fought and fought and created a space for ourselves, in our professional and social environment, so you worry about that kind of thing.

AMRITA: I really want to take a moment to laud your courage, you've touched upon so many things in that kind of opening statement, I want to say thank you from the bottom of my heart, of course as a friend but also in terms of this movement, which is what child and adolescent psychiatrist Dr Amit Sen called it. **He said we need a movement when it comes to Mental Health and Mental Illness in India.**

And one of the things you just articulated so well, is precisely why people are so concerned about speaking out. I do hope this continues to be a safe space,

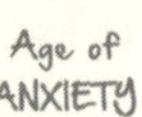

Pragya, and for anyone watching, we also do want to say, there should be no pressure to perform your story or share your story. We're all equally valid whether we share our stories or not. We have found, Pragya, when people share their stories as a first person account, it is something that helps others, right. There's something about sharing that resonates with other people. There's something about that taboo that can only be broken one by one by one by one. I know that I can just sit here on a platform and say we should all talk about it, it's very hard to do as an individual, so I really want to appreciate you doing this.

PRAGYA: Thank you again for giving me this platform, but just a very quick thing that I wanted to add there; I just want to tell people who might be listening to this that you very kindly did offer to let me tell my story anonymously, and I thought about it, and initially that's what I thought I was going to do, but then it struck me I'd rather not speak than speak anonymously, because that is just legitimising the taboo. And again I'd like to reiterate the very important point you made that just because I am speaking or I'm being called courageous on this platform for speaking up, doesn't mean that that's the only form of courage that's valid in this fight and in this struggle. Tell your story if you want to, if you're ready to, and tell it exactly the way you want to and (to) who you want to.

AMRITA: Absolutely, couldn't say it better myself. What we do want to say above all is that whatever people are going

through, they're not alone, and you know, hopefully they will take some comfort from this. I realise we jumped straight into it without giving too much context to people who are not privy to our conversations. We have been working on stories of mental health and mental illness on *The Health Collective* as I mentioned, for about 4 years now, from an India lens. We're also working on a series of books looking at collecting stories, both from a first person account, whether they're written, told or through comics, and through expert columns trying to broaden that perspective.

I want to kick off the actual interview, Pragya, by saying, there are many ways we talk about anxiety. It's entered our vocabulary in the mainstream, in a way that you know, I'm stressed, I'm anxious, I'm tense, there's that kind of lay-person understanding of anxiety, and of course there's Anxiety as a disorder.

Let me ask you when you first discovered you had Anxiety, how did you learn you had it, and what was that journey like?

PRAGYA: A quick background, some of what I might say or all of what I might say, as a prelude to this might sound slightly immodest, but I think that it is important contextually. I was always a sort of overperforming child. I have to say, I was very lucky to grow up in an environment where there was actually no pressure on me. My parents were sort of like, 'Why do you even go to school? You can just study at home.' They were really chill people, they didn't care what marks I got or grade I got.

It's odd when a child, an only child, growing up in that environment, feels the need to... I was a class topper, I topped every semester, every class, I was the best person in dance school, I was really good at sports. That's just who I was, I did

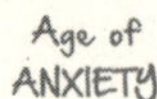

a billion things growing up. And then when I went to college, I was studying law, but I also wanted to be a journalist, and I also wanted to be in theatre. I was constantly doing a million things, and doing them well, relatively well, it took me a very, very long time to realise that this drive to be constantly working, to constantly do more and more and more with my time is actually a form of anxiety, a sort positive manifestation of anxiety.

Again, growing up in an environment where there were no expectations attached to these things, it wasn't as if I was driven by a fear of failure or the fear of... you know, trying to prove myself. It was just something that came from inside me that compelled me to constantly do a million things. I didn't see it as Anxiety, I didn't see it as a form of an Anxiety Disorder and, um, I always performed the best under pressure, and I made sure I was always under pressure, I mean I couldn't take a second off. **There were early manifestations, and I think the only negative manifestation I remember of anxiety growing up, was a little bit of separation anxiety.** I would get very anxious when my father was away. And again, these things are sort of brushed over because you're a child, you're the only daughter, you're the only child, you're obviously very attached to your father, everyone was like, she's so attached to her father. I remember it as not being usual, and he was away a lot for work. I think that carried well into adulthood and I had separation anxiety for people I loved and cared for. But other than that, there was no manifestation of it being any sort of a negative force in my life.

Cut to 2018, which is very, very recent, of course. I had a family incident, where I had just come out of a stressful job situation and I found out that my father had been subject to some fraudulent transactions and he'd lost a lot of his savings. This was the kind of situation in which I would typically perform well, under this kind of pressure. Previously I've had my father being very ill, having heart issues, me being in Delhi or Bombay, I've organised everything, made sure he got the best treatment, I just come into myself when there's pressure. But this time I just couldn't. It was the onset of what I would call the dark side of the functional Anxiety that I've been living with. It took me a good three to four months to acknowledge that this is not something I could take care of by myself.

At the risk of going on and on, there's two parts to it. **One is understanding that this is different from what I usually feel. And the second is this acknowledgement that I need help.** I have never been the kind of person who says I need help. I again am blessed with a lot of great friends and family, and I love on the kindness of friends and strangers, as much as anyone else does. To my mind, my own self-image is that I can handle everything.

And the third thing was acknowledging that if I do not address this, it is not simply the fact that it might impact my relationships or my work, it will definitely physically start to make me ill. That mind–body connection. All of what is going on in your head is actually being pumped into your body. Putting it very unscientifically, but it starts to have ramifications. I think these three realisations took me a couple of months, and that's when I realised I need to seek help.

AMRITA: Let's get a little bit into that journey of healing, what helped you? Was it therapy? Were you able to find somebody to talk to professionally? How did that work?

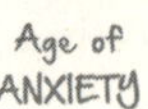

PRAGYA: I have to say something for people who are reading this, I have to caveat whatever I'm about to tell you, you will have to find your own way out of Anxiety and Depression.

There are no formulae that anybody can hand over to you.

Most of the people I know have been in therapy and that's really helped them. I was one of those people who did not respond to Therapy at all. I tried and I tried and I tried a whole bunch of different therapists, the biggest names in Delhi and Bombay I was referred to. For the longest time I thought something was wrong with me, I was not responding to therapy or whatever. There could be a longer version of this answer but in the interest of brevity, it just did not work for me.

This does not mean that I am saying that therapy doesn't work, or there's something wrong with therapy; I have seen it help my friends tremendously, tremendously. But it just didn't work for me. So the key here, and the reason I'm saying this out loud, is that if something that works for everyone else does not work for you, it's important you don't begin to think that there's something wrong with you or that this is incurable. You have to cut your losses and move on to the next thing. The next thing for me was medication, which I was super resistant about.

At the end of the day, my only real capital in life (we all come from middle class backgrounds), that I have is my brain, and you are terrified, in the line of work I'm in... it's all I use.

You are terrified of anything altering your brain in any way. You've heard horror stories of people who were on medication, etc. And then again, I went to a couple of different psychiatrists, and whatever, was prescribed, I went off it within a week, it just wasn't working for me and I was resistant, I was terrified. And then I found that the person who made the most sense and understood me was my GP – this was also a friend, a family friend. I finally went on the medication he prescribed to me, they were very low doses, I was on medication for about 6 months. It didn't make me lose my faculties in any way, it didn't make me a zombie – psychiatric drugs have come a long way from what they used to be, but yes, it's important to find a doctor who will pay attention, understand who you are and work with you, so the kind of dosage and the medication you are being given is exactly for you, and sort of helps you to pick yourself up and gets you out of the situation, rather than freezes you in a kind of numbness in that situation.

And yes, if anything, I'm much more functional than I ever was. If you want to try it, I know there's still so much resistance when it comes to medication, but it's not worth what you're losing in the bargain.

AMRITA: One of the important points is just demystifying how it works, so thank you for that. And of course as Pragya said, this isn't prescriptive, there's no one-size-fits-all remedy, none of this is meant to tell you how to live your life; we are hoping that hearing multiple stories or multiple points of view will help anyone reading this realise that they are not alone, that there are people who are qualified to help.

☺ ☺ ☺

What does it feel like to have Anxiety? And how difficult was it for you (to go

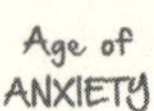

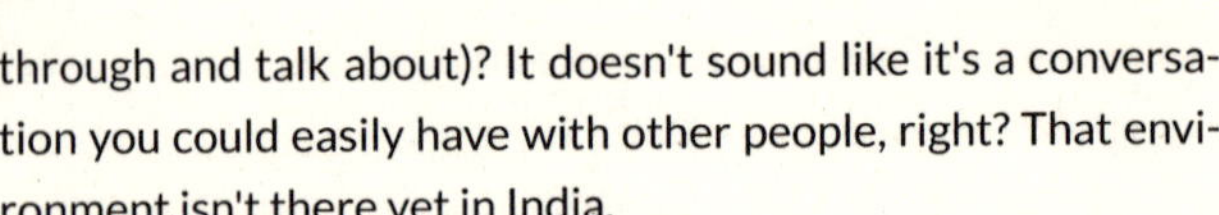

through and talk about)? It doesn't sound like it's a conversation you could easily have with other people, right? That environment isn't there yet in India.

PRAGYA: What does it feel like? It depends again, everybody has different kinds of manifestations of Anxiety. I would encourage you, there are wonderful books out there that have been written, there are blogs, there's just a lot of help available online, so read other people's accounts of Anxiety, maybe you won't relate with mine, maybe you'll relate with someone else's.

For me, it was really like the most extreme and primitive form of fight or flight syndrome, where it felt like constantly being suspended from the edge of a cliff. Again, I'm somebody who has a fair degree of mental control, so it was like, the feeling was physical. If I had a conversation with my mind, nothing was wrong. But physically I felt ill. And this is what a lot of people don't realise about Anxiety and Depression. They often manifest themselves as equally if not more as physical symptoms than just mental symptoms. And that was happening a lot to me. **It was just a terrible feeling in the pit of your stomach, of feeling constantly nervous and full of dread and fear, and paralysed by it.** Again, because I'm a highly functional person I could push through. But it meant that all of my energy was simply consumed by putting up a façade of enjoying the things that I actually enjoy, which is like maybe having a conversation like this, or doing my work, or writing or going out with friends. So I don't know if that's even halfway articulate, because this

is really not easy to describe as an experience but that's what roughly it felt like.

The second part of your question — the worst part about it is not now when I'm sort of in control of the situation and I'm talking about it. I think the most difficult part of it is being able to explain what you're experiencing when you're going through it. Because, again, like you said at the beginning, things like Anxiety or Depression, they're such a big part of parlance, right, I'm stressed about the case tomorrow, I'm stressed about the meeting tomorrow. Even your loved ones, even though they really love you and adore you and support you, sometimes are like *'What's the big deal, calm down'*.

You have to understand most people in day-to-day life are going through a lot of stress, going through a lot of tumult in their own way, so you suddenly find yourself very alone despite the fact that you have friends and you have people who you can talk to. And it's a fear of what you're feeling. You are afraid of... It's a betrayal of your mind and body, and it's very difficult, because those have been your best allies in your life. That feeling is very difficult to deal with.

It's weird, but Anxiety and Depression bring along a lot of other emotions that are also negative and toxic that you have to deal with. So yeah, it's a perfect storm, but definitely one that you can get out of.

AMRITA: Were there reactions that were helpful along the way even before you found your footing? Was there anything you want to call out? Because often I think we don't know how to be — as allies, friends, families, caregivers... was there anything that you found helpful?

PRAGYA: So, I have to say this, and at the risk of repeating myself, I have the

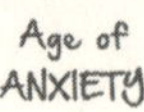

best set of friends and supporters that anyone, any girl, any human being could ask for. This was the toughest part of having to deal with Anxiety. Whatever problems I have had to deal with in life I have gotten through because I have such incredible friends and such an incredible support system. This was the first time that support system failed me. And not because of any fault of theirs, every single friend of mine who knows about this or knew about this tried to help me in whatever way they could.

Somehow, and I'm fortunate I got to the point that this one time I'm going to have to find the solutions myself, I cannot outsource them.

Everything that people were telling me – almost all the people close to me, and I really hope that if they are reading this they understand I'm saying this with all the love for them – almost everyone was like, 'You just need to come back to work and you'll be fine'.

I was horrified by that suggestion – I'm nothing but my work. That was just really... (well not nothing, but it's a really big part of my life). Then there were people who said things like 'You need to do more yoga, you need to do more this', 'You need to do meditation', and 'You need to find natural ways of doing this', and... and obviously they all meant well. This sounds like perfectly reasonable advice. **But what happens when you are going through Anxiety is that all these inputs are making you**

all the more anxious.

Because you're suddenly like, *'I should be doing this, I should be doing that'*. And somewhere you are constantly feeling, you cannot help but feeling that this is something you have brought on yourself, that you have done this to yourself. And it's not true. You have not done this to yourself any more than you can give yourself — of course you can prevent things and treat things. It's like any other illness, you can't give yourself cancer, you cannot give yourself tuberculosis. That's not what you do. And that's the same with Anxiety. It did not help me, whatever I was hearing from friends, and that was making me feel alone and resentful, until I realised I have to find the solutions, and I did. It was just a series of experimentations.

And the only thing I can really say is do not — and it sounds so cliched but it's really the only take-away you can have, because whatever I'm telling you otherwise will not fit in to your life, your pattern, but what will for sure — do not give up, trust that the answers will come. **Try meditation, if it doesn't work, screw it. Try therapy, maybe dancing will work. Whatever works, just work with yourself.**

And take the help of medication, if you need to. I'm saying this again, because people very close to me said things to me like, 'I know somebody who started taking medication and she never got off it', or 'he never got off it, he went crazy' and 'she was a vegetable', and 'she drank with her medication so she died very early'. None of these things happened to me. I enjoy my wine very much and I enjoy my martinis very much. I did not become less functional, I did not become addicted, I did not... nothing bad happened. I am sane, in all the possible ways that I want to be sane.

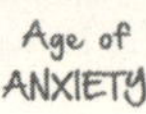

AMRITA: Right now, what we are living through, we are going through a completely unprecedented crisis, a year where, I've been told in an interview, if people are not feeling anxious, they're not paying attention. This was Professor Steve Joordens, actually who has a short course 'Mind Control', on how to deal with what's going on with Anxiety and Covid-19.

One of the things that I also hear from your story is that it's so hard to deal with precisely because you feel you're the only one going through it. Do you think it would have been helpful to know, maybe by name, maybe by story, to know other people who are struggling but finding their own feet, finding their own way?

PRAGYA: Absolutely. And I sought that out. It's so funny but having gone through it, I suddenly began to see things I hadn't seen before in the sense that I began to see friends of mine who probably had underlying Anxiety or depressive disorders who were not addressing it, and I made up my mind that once I'm through with this, I'm going to bring it up with them and I did.

So it made me see it in other people even if they were not seeing it within themselves, and getting to know friends is something, you get to know them so intimately, you know them so closely that you don't see them as outside yourself, so objectivity is hard to come by. This gave me that momentary objective lens to look at their issues and their problems. So that was one thing. It's also really important, it isn't difficult to find

accounts of Anxiety, people talking about it.

Like you said, like we've been saying, it's not very common but it's not uncommon to come across some resource for it. You have to find what speaks to you. A lot of accounts did not make sense to me. I think everything is very particular and peculiar as well as very generalised. It's important to keep reading and looking for stuff till it starts making sense to you. It's the same thing I was saying earlier as finding the 'cure' or finding the management process. You just have to find what works for you; you have to trust that there are so many possibilities, there are so many tools available to you. The whole world is your oyster. It's not just medication and therapy. It's a billion things out there and you don't know what's going to help you but something will.

Once it does — this sounds very cliched and I'm a very cynical person — there is a before and after. There is so much that you don't realise that you've been storing in your body and storing in your mind, that gets flushed in the process of flushing out Anxiety, that you're born again. So if this feels like the end of the world, then it is, but it's the end of a world that you don't want to be in anymore.

AMRITA: How has this year (2020) been for you? It's a year where all of a sudden everyone is talking about anxiety and there's a very clear link between what we're seeing and going through, we're able to make sense of the anxiety and what's causing it in a way that might not have been possible if it weren't such an 'era-defining' year. How have you been? How are you feeling?

PRAGYA: It's interesting, like you said, you have to be anxious in this moment. Some people have it worse than others, but... it's as close to doomsday as we've seen as a civilisation I suppose. So obviously there are triggers and people who

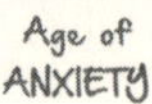

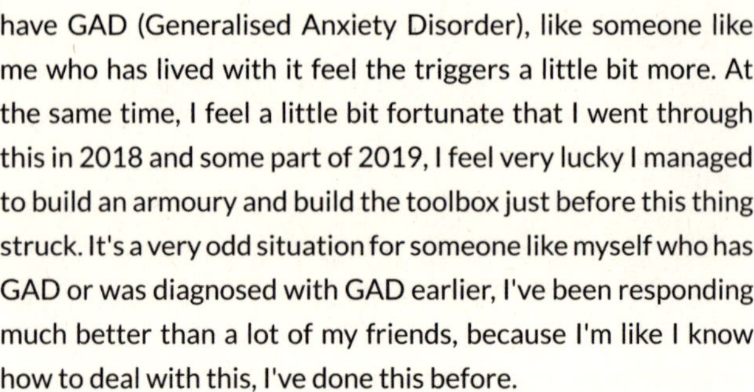

have GAD (Generalised Anxiety Disorder), like someone like me who has lived with it feel the triggers a little bit more. At the same time, I feel a little bit fortunate that I went through this in 2018 and some part of 2019, I feel very lucky I managed to build an armoury and build the toolbox just before this thing struck. It's a very odd situation for someone like myself who has GAD or was diagnosed with GAD earlier, I've been responding much better than a lot of my friends, because I'm like I know how to deal with this, I've done this before.

It's also a weird kind of blessing that I have had this experience before. I think it's great that we are at a time that everyone is going through this, which means there is some sort of great equaliser... (though nothing is a great equaliser beyond a certain point) to some extent. Hopefully it will open up channels to acknowledge what they are going through and maybe make it less of a taboo. Hope against hope.

AMRITA: That's quite beautiful. Do you have a message for your younger self or pre-2018 Pragya or anyone who is reading and putting two and two together, what would that message be?

PRAGYA: Don't do a thing differently. Live your life exactly like you want to live it, whatever happens, you have the ability to deal with it and you will.

AMRITA: That's beautiful, It's really moving you were able to share this, that you're trying to help lift the taboo, we have to do this as individuals, isn't it... we have to do this together.

PRAGYA: Like you, like myself, if you're reading this and feel like reaching out, or writing to me, I'm on Twitter and around, Amrita can connect you, whatever, just write, call, message... I'm happy to have a chat and listen, if it helps at all. Thank you.

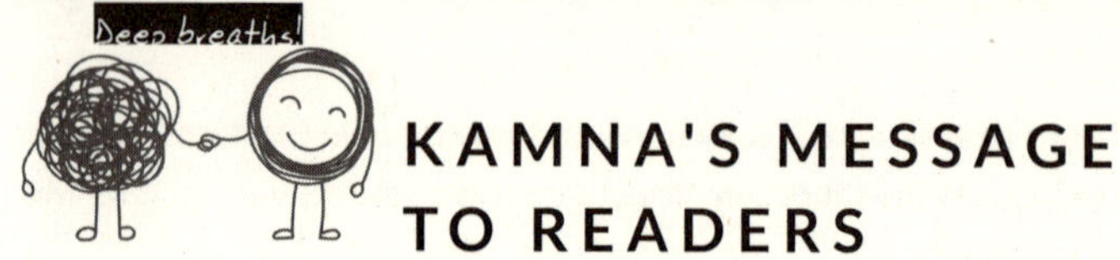

KAMNA'S MESSAGE TO READERS

Being diagnosed and living with a mental health illness brings with it many challenges. Here are some important things that will help decode how to address the problem of Anxiety Disorders from multiple vantage points:

- An Anxiety Disorder can manifest in many different ways. The way you experience it can and will be different from the way another person does.
- There will be many questions that will arise in your mind as you struggle to come to terms with a diagnosis. This struggle is normal and it is important to know and understand how you feel as you keep taking steps towards self-care and treatment options.
- There is no one-size-fits-all solution that would be applicable in the treatment of Anxiety Disorders, as is the case for other mental health related problems too.
- Experiencing anxiety across situations that are difficult and challenging is a normal experience. As we are going through situations like the current pandemic, or if we were to be trapped in a situation like a flood or a tsunami, mental health related problems are likely to emerge.
- A mental health problem can have an onset regardless of the individual's age, gender, socioeconomic, religious, or geographic background. The manifestations of the illness might vary but they do need to be treated.
- Engaging in caring for yourself even as you seek treatment for the Anxiety that you might be experiencing is critical.
- Surrounding yourself with friends and family members who are understanding, supportive and available to aid you in the process of working through your Anxiety is helpful.

• Reaching out for help is not a sign of weakness and does not reflect upon any deficit within who you are. Regardless of the impediments you face, do reach out and seek support in whichever way it can work for you.

MYTHS AND FACTS

Dr Bhavana Gautam has been practicing as a holistic health consultant and emotional well-being expert for close to 10 years now and is based in a Mumbai, working mainly with young adults, teens and women on issues such as Anxiety, Depression, lifestyle disease management and stress management. She shared some Myths and Facts with Sukanya Sharma for The Health Collective *and readers of this book.*

Myth: Anxiety is the same as worry

Fact: While anxiety and worry are used interchangeably quite frequently, they have different implications in the way they are experienced. Short term worry about a crisis or a difficulty is in fact normal and can even help with finding suitable solutions or performance improvement. It's only when it becomes persistent, excessive, irrational or debilitating that we identify it as Anxiety Disorder.

Myth: Medication is the perfect way to get rid of Anxiety

Fact: There is enough evidence today that the best approach to support management of Anxiety Disorders is via a therapy component and via pharmacology (or medicine component) especially when there are significant Anxiety symptoms. While medication helps at the stage of acute distress or panic attacks, it is only a long-term combination effect with psychotherapy and medication that

can help to systematically convert irrational anxiety evoking thoughts into rational productive emotions. Today, mindfulness, meditation with appropriate nutrition support are also being used extensively in the management of Anxiety.

Myth: Panic attacks are the same as Anxiety

Fact: Panic attacks are sudden extreme feelings of fear or terror and may even mimic a heart attack (chest pain, shortness of breath, excessive sweating), that's how severe the physical symptoms are. Panic attacks may occur suddenly or unexpectedly and typically last for a few minutes. Not everyone who has Anxiety will experience a panic attack.

Myth: Children do not experience Anxiety, they just worry

Fact: All children experience strong emotions as their world seems so overwhelming or uncertain to them. The nervousness of separation from parents, or worry about starting a new school are common scenarios. However if the child doesn't seem to outgrow the issue or the fear and worry interfere with their everyday functioning it could be a matter of concern. Anxiety disorders have been found to be one of the most common mental health disorders in children and adolescents and are rising in prevalence (on the CDC site,[19] it's reported that about 7.1% of children aged 3–17 years have diagnosed Anxiety). In fact, most young adults with Anxiety Disorder will report having displayed the symptoms at some point in their childhood.

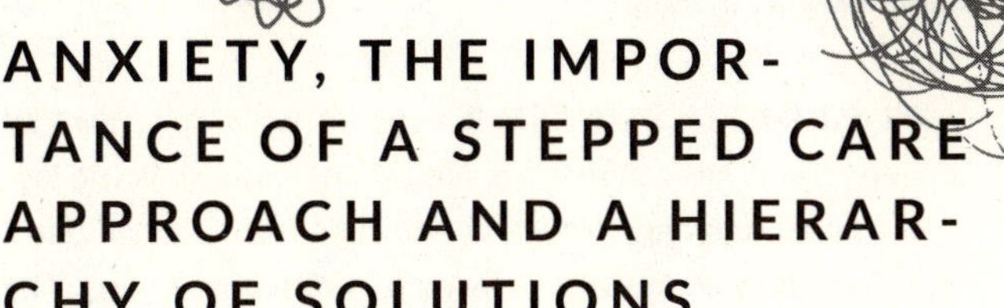

ANXIETY, THE IMPORTANCE OF A STEPPED CARE APPROACH AND A HIERARCHY OF SOLUTIONS

An Interview with Dr Soumitra Pathare

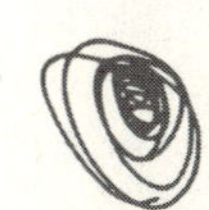

Dr Soumitra Pathare is a Consultant Psychiatrist at Ruby Hall Clinic, Pune, and Director, Centre for Mental Health Law and Policy. He trained at Seth Gordhandas Sunderdas Medical College and King Edward Memorial Hospital, Mumbai and Guy's and St Thomas' Hospitals Medical School, London. He is interested in mental health policy and legislation and service development, and is based in Pune. He tweets @netshrink.

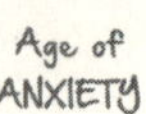

AMRITA: What is the scope of the problem when we talk about Anxiety in India?

DR SOUMITRA PATHARE: It depends what you mean by anxiety, (as) it has too many connotations — there is the layman's understanding of anxiety and there's also a clinician's understanding of Anxiety. They're two different things. The layman's understanding of anxiety very often is to do with even normal stuff, you know, like 'I have an exam coming up and I'm anxious.' Now that's called anxiety too, whereas when clinicians talk about anxiety, they're talking about abnormal Anxiety; they're not talking about these normal things.

When laypeople talk about anxiety it's stuff that is a natural response, it's a survival response. If you are in front of a tiger, you'll feel anxious — that's a normal reaction your body is designed for... I'm dumbing this down, but abnormal anxiety is when you feel anxious even where there is no tiger in front of you, you know, and there's no reason to feel anxious. That's a very simplistic way of looking at it.

So clinicians when they say Anxiety, they actually mean abnormal stuff. I think the general population when they mean anxiety, mean the normal stuff. **If I'm feeling anxious about the fact that I might get Covid, that's a reasonable anxiety to have at this point in time.**

It's only if that anxiety gets to a point where it stops me from functioning or it makes my life so miserable that I can't do anything, then you can say it's become abnormal in some sort of way. It's important to distinguish what people call anxiety and what clinicians call Anxiety.

AMRITA: That helps as a starting point. If we talk about what people are calling anxiety, as you said right now during this pandemic, it's normal to be anxious or to worry. We've been hearing about this uptick in stress and anxiety and I suppose fear as well — these are not technical terms. Are you seeing that in practice as well, that more people think they're anxious? Leaving the disorder aside for a moment.

DR SOUMITRA PATHARE: That I think is quite obvious, not just in practice even in general conversation, you realise people are anxious. There are many things to be anxious about. A lot of the anxiety is actually because of uncertainty. People are uncertain whether their jobs will survive or not survive. That creates uncertainty.

Any uncertainty in human beings does create anxiety. You know, '*I don't know whether my job is going to be there in 3 months time, or not be there*', '*I have loans to pay*', '*I have kids to put through school*'. It's quite understandable that you would then have job anxiety, financial anxiety.

If you're a young person in college, you don't know whether your college is going to restart or not, when is it going to restart, how is it going to interfere with your education? That can reasonably cause anxiety. I think if you ask anybody, there would be reasonable grounds why almost every individual would have reasons for anxiety. There's health-related anxiety, education-related anxiety, it's

probably even just broadly future-related anxiety. What's going to happen to the world? These are worries that people will have. So you do see a lot more anxiety, I have no doubt about that.

The problem with anxiety is that we are all designed for dealing with anxiety as a short burst, so using the tiger example, you are used to dealing with having seen a tiger and run away from there — the fight or flight response that is there, and then that ends. But if the tiger is staring at you every minute, all the time, then our bodies are not designed, our minds are not designed to deal with that kind of, 'Oh my god the tiger is in front of me all the time'.

What happens really is that if you have even normal anxiety that goes on for too long, then that can lead to both physical health and mental health problems. Physical problems, obviously, and mental problems too.

So it's not that people aren't anxious, the real issue is how long is that anxiety going to go on. We all have different levels of resilience. We all can cope with stress (if I can use it in a very very broad sense of the term) in varying amounts, and when our limits are reached, then that pushes us into some form of illness, either physical or mental. Anxiety going on for long is probably what is the worry.

AMRITA: What would you say to someone who worries that

they or someone in their family is anxious. You said that it's a cause for worry when it's impeding your day-to-day function, or very extreme...

DR PATHARE: That's right.

AMRITA: What would your advice be to someone right now, in the pandemic where everything is quite virtual anyway?

DR PATHARE: I think one of the best ways to reduce anxiety — we are talking at a population level (rather than an individual, personal level) — one of the best ways to reduce anxiety for many people, is to reduce uncertainty.

If we can reduce uncertainty, that will reduce anxiety. So advice to employers would be, why don't you reduce uncertainty for your employees? And while you might not have definitive answers, there is a lot of uncertainty that can be reduced. You can tell your employees this is where we are at, this is what is going to happen in 3 months; we don't know anything beyond 3 months but if xyz happens after 3 months then abc will happen to people. You know, some kind of a metric that people can then use, and gives you a sense of control over the situation, you have some degree of certainty.

Or in the education space, for example if the government was to provide some certainties like saying no exams this year till December, that's a certain degree of certainty. Once you have that certainty, you tend to relax to some extent, because you know that ok nothing is going to happen till that point in time. Even if it's not a great result, you at least have that certainty. I think one of the broadest things that we can do, is to try and ask ourselves, how can we reduce uncertainty? What are the certainties we can bring about? That helps to control or at least

keep your anxiety under control. That's the broad advice to everybody.

And now I know people will say, *'But a lot of these uncertainties are not in my hand, what am I going to do about it?'* In which case actually then it's a good idea to ask yourself, *'Which of these things that are worrying me are things under my control and which are not under my control? And the things that are under my control, what am I going to do about them so that it reduces my anxiety?'*

So take the example of a student — *'I don't know when exams will happen'*. The easiest thing may be to tell yourself might be even if exams are happening this year, I'm taking a break, I'm going to tell myself I'm taking a gap year. And that's completely fine, I don't have to worry for 12 months. I'll worry about next year and I'll start my education again, like it is one year, a gap year. That helps you have certainty even if you don't have control over what's not in your control.

So I think people need those kinds of certainties, I think certainties help to reduce anxiety. That's a very broad thing. There's other stuff like, *'Why don't you do some meditation and some prananyam and exercise'* — of course those are things that help you to control your anxiety, but fundamentally a lot of the anxiety arises out of uncertainty, so try and get over the uncertainty is probably what you want to do.

AMRITA: And where do you — of course you would diagnose

in a certain way — where would you be concerned that someone should come in or at least even virtually talk to a therapist or a psychiatrist for a diagnosis that it might be an Anxiety Disorder? Where does that line get crossed?

DR PATHARE: That's a simple thing: Imagine if it starts interfering with your bodily functions for example. What I mean by bodily functions — as in, you're not able to sleep well, you get up in the morning, you're tired, you're not able to concentrate on anything, you're not able to do your day-to-day activities.

You have distress to the level where the distress becomes disabling now, you know you can't get your mind off it at all. Or let's say, you lose your appetite, for example, you're not eating, you're losing weight. **Those are the kinds of things you want to say, ok should I probably talk to somebody... either a psychologist or a counsellor or a psychiatrist.** A simple metric would be, that either it is interfering with your functioning, your physical functioning or your activities of day-to-day living, or if it is causing distress to the point where you're not able to bear with the distress. We're all able to live with a certain amount of distress. Some distress which just goes out of control, and when you reach that point where your distress is now out of control; you can't do anything but think of that thing all day, then maybe that's when you need to actually say ok I'm going to go and talk to someone.

AMRITA: I do want to ask you, we're obviously speaking in English and we've had some conversations on privilege and this bubble we're in. What are some of the colloquial terms people would use for Anxiety or if you want to talk of common Mental Health or Mental Illness terms that come up?

DR PATHARE: I think the commonest thing that people seem to understand

are 'stress' and 'tension'. You say 'tension' in India and everyone understands. If you go to the rural parts of the country, and you say, '*tension hain bahut*', they understand. What that translates to is that they are anxious about something or they're stressed about something.

Things like stress and tension, are words that although English, are understood by people who don't speak English. It's just like 'mobile', you know, you can go and say mobile anywhere in India, everyone knows what 'mobile' is, even though it's not a Hindi word. In fact, if you spoke the exact translation in Sanskritised Hindi, which I don't even know what it is, most people would stare at you blankly.

What we found in our work in rural areas is that the metaphor they understand or words they understand is stress and tension... easily understood by the average person.

AMRITA: Two linked questions: In the last two-and-a-half decades that you have been practising, are you seeing more interest in mental health and illness from the mainstream as well. Are you seeing more people talking about things like anxiety? The disclaimer being that the title of the book is *Age of Anxiety*, something I used to make fun of, but it does feel like we are living in an Age of Anxiety! Is it because we are talking about it more? Or are we genuinely more stressed or there is more tension? Maybe we should call it Age of Tension, based on what you just told me. Are we feeling it more, talking about it more,

or is it actually an increase?

DR PATHARE: Firstly let's split that sentence into many parts.

The first is, who is the 'we'? I think the 'we' in this context very often tends to be a certain urbanised section of our society, and even that urbanised section is probably, if I were to use very narrow terms like upper class, upper socio-economic classes or middle class. You know the woman who comes to cook at my place or our maid, probably doesn't think about anxiety as such, that's not her concern. It's a concern for a certain set of people. If you go to rural areas, they do have Anxiety and tension, they are not concerned about Anxiety and tension, they are primarily concerned about the reasons for that Anxiety and tension. So the concerns will be around things like, '*My crops are not doing well this year*', for example, or '*I have a financial difficulty*' or '*There's domestic abuse in the house and I'm worried about...*' they don't articulate it as an anxiety, they articulate it as the reason why they are feeling like that.

It's a question of who articulates it in which way. I think the Age of Anxiety as you said, is articulated largely by a certain urbanised section of our society, not everybody.

That is something you need to kind of distinguish between.

Are we seeing more of it was (also) your question. If I can take you back to the Maslow kind of hierarchy... There's a hierarchy of needs, as your needs at the lower level get satisfied, you start worrying about a higher level of needs. The peak level of that pyramid that Maslow talks about are things like self-actualisation. You don't get to that peak of self-actualisation till you satisfy your lower

level needs.

I think you can almost say that depending on where people are on that Maslow's hierarchy of needs, that's where they would be. Your primary needs are food, shelter, clothing, well even before food shelter clothing, you have survival, you want to ensure you just survive, you don't die. Then food, shelter, clothing, and then there's some other things, then probably you come to things like Anxiety and Depression, and then you might go to worrying about the world and then you worry about yourself and self-actualisation and the meaning of life.

So I think what happens is, you see Anxiety on that hierarchy of needs. As populations move up on that hierarchy of needs, you'll see more and more of certain things happening. If all your lower level needs are met, you then worry about higher level needs. I think it's an indication. It's not a question of are we seeing more or less of it. If we're seeing more of it in a certain group, then clearly their lower level needs have been met so they're now worrying about it. If you're not seeing a lot of it in some other groups, then their lower level needs have not yet been met, so they're not worrying about it.

AMRITA: You've clarified anxiety, layperson and clinicians' understanding of it, Maslow's hierarchy. What are some of the other concerns during this pandemic? You've been outspoken about some of them, you've also said we need to stop looking at some of these as individual concerns, but much wider, social...

DR PATHARE: That's my point. **I think a pandemic is a good example of something that, irrespective of your coping strategies, you're going to get swamped with. So you might be very good at coping with things, you might deal with many issues, but a pandemic is like a wave which just washes over you, however good your skills might be.**

It's a bit like when you have a flood, however strong your building might be, or what you've done, a flood will bring down the best of buildings around it. And so a pandemic in that sense, is increasingly that kind of thing, it's an environmental event which swamps all individual differences. And so that has been the reason why I have been saying we should stop looking at individuals and look at environmental and social factors because this is such a huge event that it completely swamps everything else. I think it's such a thing that even people with good coping skills, lots of resilience and lots of support are still going to get swamped with this pandemic. It seems to me that focusing on individuals then seems like a... you know it's a bit like saying this building was built better because it withstood the flood and the other one didn't, but a flood is a flood and is going to swamp everyone. It's like a — I hate to use the word — tsunami, a wave that washes all over you. How strong you are or not almost becomes irrelevant then.

☺☺☺

AMRITA: You've spoken in the past about dealing with Anxiety and Depression yourself... can you share anything with our readers?

DR PATHARE: I returned to India (after leaving my academic position at a UK university) in 1999 with the intention of working at a public sector hospital or

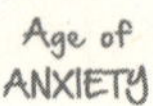

medical school. I tried doing this for a year and it was an utter nightmare — I was given short term contracts, initially for 6 months, then 3 months, and the final straw, when I was offered a 28-day contract, I left. I had nothing in hand at the time, I was 35 years old with a 3-year-old kid and no other source of income.

The next 6 months, I was at a loss when it came to what to do. I had left everything I had in the UK and returned to India, and I had nothing to do here. I did not want to return to the UK either. I was also running out of my savings and money. That was a very, very stressful period and although I did not seek any professional help, I do know that I was clinically depressed. I did entertain suicidal thoughts to the extent that my wife was extremely worried about my safety. I was not actively suicidal, but I did go to bed each night, hoping I did not get up in the morning. I also remember saying to my wife that I wouldn't mind if I got run over by a bus or truck. I wasn't going to actively attempt anything, but was in a passive way hoping it would end. I do remember the sense of being a failure.

(Editor's Note: If you or anyone you know mentions feeling distressed or suicidal, please reach out to a professional for help. We have shared third-party helplines at the end of this book.)

I was unable to work at all — the energy had gone out of me. I usually spent the entire day either gardening or doing simple tasks, for e.g., painting the fence, etc. I also gave up my PhD

which was about 3 months from completion.

I think I finally just got out of it – largely because depression for most people is a self-limiting condition. The one and only help I had was my wife's support. I also had to dig deep into my own resources. I was determined that I was not going to quit and die when I was down and out. I then decided to get back to work and started working at a local general hospital as a visiting consultant psychiatrist. Over time, things improved and 20 years down the road, I have much to be satisfied about.

☺ ☺ ☺

AMRITA: If we had to sum up, and the caveat being there are so many new players in this space, no certification process (for counsellors in India, etc.), people are vulnerable and feel they might need to reach out, how do you advise, who do we reach out to, if we need to?

DR PATHARE: Give everyone the benefit of doubt, I think potentially most people who are doing something to help other people are well-intentioned. Now, unfortunately the road to hell is paved with good intentions, so that doesn't necessarily translate into good outcomes for anybody, but the fact is nobody is questioning anybody's intentions.

Having put that aside, I think what we should be doing is think of a hierarchy of solutions.

Just like you think of a hierarchy of needs, it's a good idea to think of a hierarchy of solutions. What is the lowest base level in that hierarchy? The base level of that hierarchy is offering, giving people a lot of skills for self-care. I think self-

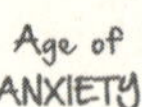

care is probably the best thing. What can I do to help myself?

And that's probably the base of the pyramid. It's the cheapest, if you thought of a pyramid in terms of availability and cost, self-care is at the bottom of it... it's the cheapest, it doesn't cost a lot. And it's also something that's easily available, because all of us can do self-care. So there are a lot of simple self-care things the government can be promoting and putting it out, which they have been doing, but not in a systematic sort of manner. I think we should really focus our attention on promoting self-care, because that is probably the best thing we can do for large numbers of people, given our population, if you can build up people's self-care.

Imagine if you had like a filtering system — self-care acts like one, lowest level of filter, which probably takes care of the largest chunk of people.

And then people who slip through that filter because self-care is not working, they need something more, then they should probably reach out to an informal level of care as we call it, informal counsellors or people, not formally trained in psychological interventions but they're probably somebody like you, for example, who has an interest, who likes to help people, who might undergo a week-long or two-week-long training just to understand some basics and is then able to talk and help others. And again that's a huge number of people you can recruit into that informal caring. And then that acts as another filter.

And then you have another filter beyond that, like semi-formal services, like helplines you can call up. Your informal network might be your friends and family, but if that's not working, then maybe you call a helpline, and that's the next level of filter.

And then people who can't be helped beyond that level of filter, well the helpline, you tried calling and you need something more, then probably you can get help from professional services, that could be trained psychologists, counsellors and even psychiatrists.

I would see this as a kind of graded approach, rather than say, everybody should go to the psychiatrist or the counsellor. Firstly, everybody doesn't need it, and secondly you'll just swamp the system. You'll swamp the system with the ones who are the most demanding, not necessarily the ones who are most needy. When you swamp the system, and there's too many people and too few resources, then how do you triage? The only triage that ends up happening is the ones who shout the loudest get the most of it, but that does not equate to the most needy. Sometimes the most needy stand at the back of the queue quietly because they don't even know how to get help.

I think what we should be promoting is this kind of a very, what clinicians tend to refer to, as a stepped care approach.

You do that with physical health also, if you have a cough and cold, you don't rush off to see the chest physician. If you get a cough and cold, you're probably going to try some grandmother's remedies at home, you know what generally works for you. And if that doesn't work, after 4–5 days, you might get a little concerned and you might ask a few friends around, saying, listen that cough is

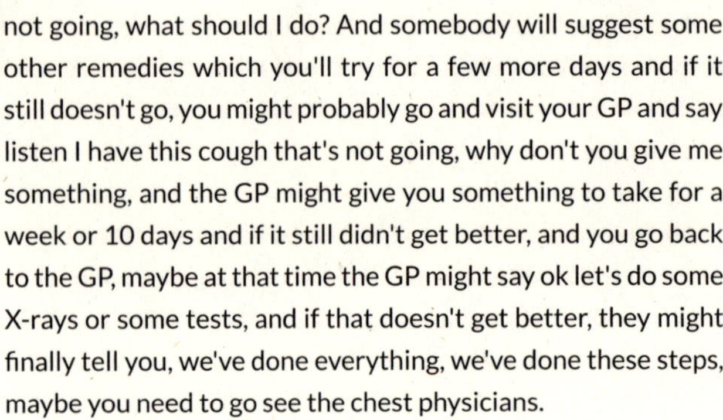

not going, what should I do? And somebody will suggest some other remedies which you'll try for a few more days and if it still doesn't go, you might probably go and visit your GP and say listen I have this cough that's not going, why don't you give me something, and the GP might give you something to take for a week or 10 days and if it still didn't get better, and you go back to the GP, maybe at that time the GP might say ok let's do some X-rays or some tests, and if that doesn't get better, they might finally tell you, we've done everything, we've done these steps, maybe you need to go see the chest physicians.

It's a graded approach you've got and not every person ended up meeting the chest physician. The same logic needs to be applied to mental health issues. You don't want everyone with a cough ending up at a chest physician's. You don't want everyone with any level of anxiety ending up at the psychologist or a psychiatrist.

AMRITA: I hope you can help put that into practice?

DR PATHARE: We are trying to. In Gujarat where we are running Atmiyata, you know our programme. What we did during the pandemic time — Atmiyata sits at that informal care, helpline level of care, but also encourages a lot of self-care, it teaches self-care. What we did with all our Atimayata champions was to give them some additional training on specifically what are the issues that come up with the pandemic, and how to help them with those issues. And so they are there in the vil-

lage, and most of the champions say they are getting 2/3 calls in a week from people within the village asking for help, to help with xyz. So that works, and if that doesn't work, then they know how to link people to the health system, so then they say look I can help you go to the PHC (primary health care centre), there's a doctor, there who can help you, who's been trained. And so they link people to the healthcare system. We are actually doing that in practice, so it is happening, and it is quite feasible.

AMRITA: Is it a pilot?

DR PATHARE: Not a pilot, it's been running for 3–4 years now; we cover about 550-odd villages, we have close to 700 such champions who are present, so almost every village has at least 1 champion, and most of these villages will have a population of about 2000 or 3000, so we are covering about 1 million people. This is in Mehsana district in Gujarat. We are also trying to expand it, there's a small pilot which we have started along with a government agency (MAVIM), the Maharahstra government corporation which basically sets up women's self-help groups in villages. They are present in close to 12,000 villages in Maharashtra, they support about 100,000 self-help groups of women.

We are doing a small pilot with them in 100 villages, to see if we can train their people to be able to do what our champions do, so that we can run the system through their network (because they have such a wide-spread network), so in a sense piggyback our intervention onto their existing network, and using a kind of social franchising model.

We would still do the training, set quality control and all of that, but they still implement the Atmiyata program while we can still assure they are doing it at a

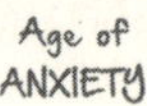

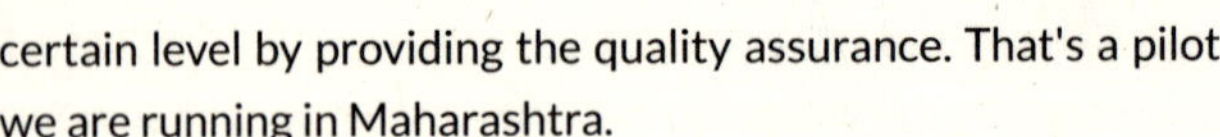

certain level by providing the quality assurance. That's a pilot we are running in Maharashtra.

We are hoping to branch out, work in other states, too — there's a lot of interest, and people are willing to put money.

AMRITA: That's really incredible.I need to read up more about these programmes and see where we can share more. (*More information is available on the Centre for Mental Health Law and Policy site.*)

UNDERSTANDING ANXIETY IN THE INDIAN CONTEXT

An Interview with Raj Mariwala

Raj Mariwala is Director, Mariwala Health Initiative, which funds various mental health-related projects in India. In this lightly edited interview, Raj shares more on the work happening via partner organisations, Mariwala Health Initiative, and some thoughts on her personal journey with Anxiety. Mariwala has an educational background in Business Economics and International Relations and has worked previously with Mercy Corps International. Currently, Raj serves on the Advisory Board of BluePrint Group, a global joint advocacy, communications, and learning coalition on mental health as well as Advisory for the Lancet Commission on Stigma and Discrimination. In line with other interests, Raj is also a Board Member of Parcham, a non-profit that serves adolescent girls through sports.

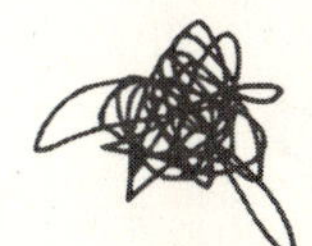

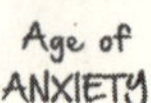

AMRITA: Can you share any details from your work or your partner organisations' work on Anxiety in India that would be useful for us to go through?

RAJ MARIWALA: We have a range of partners whose interventions on Anxiety you may find interesting in their specificity. For example, Basic Needs India did interventions on disaster relief and preparedness in areas prone to such disasters – such as Cyclone Fani and more. You can find a write up of one such programme in Bridging The Care Gap on resilience in disaster prone areas.

Our partner in Uttarakhand Burans does work around anxiety and psychosocial concerns of rural youth. iCall (a free telephone and email counselling service) has a considerable amount of work done on student Anxiety, on providing psychosocial support to those who go to the coaching capital of the world – Kota. Finally, the Sukoon project works on anxieties and other issues in family courts of Maharashtra.

AMRITA: What are some of the key findings on Anxiety in India, that you would like to comment on or share?

RAJ MARIWALA: Unfortunately, most findings I've come across are narrowly bio-medical, focused many a time in urban settings, with an epidemiological focus. Combined with that the cultural idioms of distress being glibly translated into categories such as depression and anxiety are important to unpack.

Mental health training and language comes from a Euro-American backdrop lacking mooring in local and social contexts — and this will affect the findings on Anxiety.

AMRITA: Do you think that we are living in an Age of Anxiety (disclaimer: totally the title of the book); if so, why? And if not, why not?

RAJ MARIWALA: Anxiety is an adaptive trait, or so I often tell people. Some say performance is a downturned U of performance-pressure and anxiety plays a role in whether it urges you to do better or stops you in your tracks. I think anxiety has been referred to by Hippocrates, Cicero and more such philosophers.

If you look up the etymology of the word anxiety — some say it has Latin roots, and then of course more specific French, German and old English roots. Of course, I think that there are so many chronicles — Munch's 'The Scream', or Shakespeare's *Macbeth*, 'Out damned spot' is so anxiety-provoking, not to mention the 'Age of Anxiety' is a poem by WH Auden — so I think it is inextricably linked to mammalian species.

We possibly are hearing about it more now due to diagnostic creep as well as collective global experience of a seemingly unsurmountable pandemic. Since our Anxiety doesn't operate in a vacuum — many countries globally are also facing lockdowns on freedoms, fascist crackdowns on dissent, on a right to a life without violence. Add to that climate change and broken carceral justice systems all over the world — makes me feel like this is indeed the Age of Anxiety.

AMRITA: The pandemic, lockdown 1.0, un-lockdown and many aspects have led to an uptick in mental distress, stress, anxiety and fear are not uncommon to

hear about. Can you share any of your thoughts on this, does it reflect what you're seeing or hearing about (even via, say, iCall's work?) and what are your specific concerns. What are some of the more long-term concerns and issues we need to be addressing?

RAJ MARIWALA: There is of course the discourse that anxiety during this time is 'normal'. It's amusing for me to hear this and say it too, with the full knowledge that this articulation makes my Anxiety abnormal. In terms of anxieties, there is much about contracting Covid, infecting family members with Covid or family members falling ill. Other concerns revolve around uncertainty of job, school, college, inability to plan ahead.

iCall has been fielding a very high call and email volume especially around issues of education, career, the economic crisis and general emotional distress. There is much work to be done in terms of long term ramifications as effects will last well past 2 years — especially around losses of plans, people, dreams, etc. Finally, we will need to do concerted work around suicide prevention.

AMRITA: Any myths you'd like to bust when it comes to Anxiety for one, and more broadly, mental illness in India?

RAJ MARIWALA: The approach to mental illness is still focused just on the individual rather than looking at a complex

interplay of factors which includes context and systemic issues. This is also where the idea of cure/ recovery springs from — moored in the biomedical. For example, a woman may have anxiety about her body image because everything around her is telling her that her body is wrong. Or, in a homophobic world, taking a pill for say mental illness when you may face discrimination and violence is only going to do so much.

AMRITA: Can you share a little bit about your own experience with Anxiety? When did you learn you had Anxiety, what has helped along the way?

RAJ MARIWALA: Looking back, I know I've had Anxiety as a very young child. It wasn't recognised as such either. I realised well into my adult life that my Anxiety levels weren't normal. I had Anxiety around anyone new for example (I would burst into tears), Anxiety around any interaction in play school. Apparently, you can get F's for interaction in kindergarten too. I was perceived to have a sensitive stomach, or to be prone to nausea because I would throw up during exam time. One of my earlier memories, in 2nd standard, is being made to sit outside the classroom in the corridor so I could reach the bathroom easily to throw up as I wrote the exam.

I learned that I had 'clinical' Anxiety even after I started therapy. Not sure exactly when the realisation hit, but, it was a Eureka moment to realise that not everyone wakes up with massive Anxiety even before their eyes are properly open. What has helped along the way is having control over a career that helps me with Anxiety (dog training, feline behaviour). But, also regular therapy and medication which means visiting a psychiatrist. Despite all this agency and privilege — it is still something I live with daily.

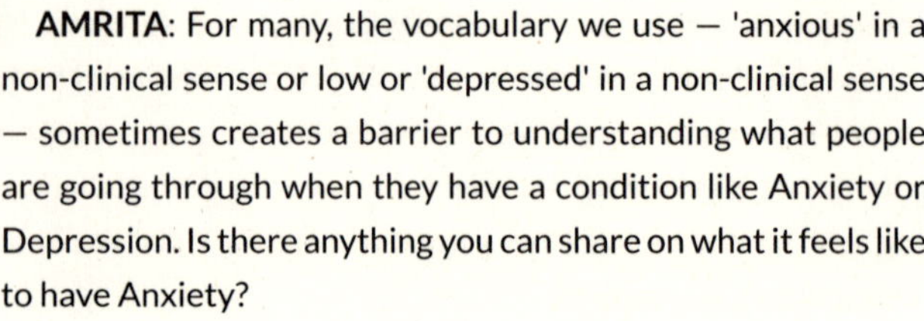

AMRITA: For many, the vocabulary we use – 'anxious' in a non-clinical sense or low or 'depressed' in a non-clinical sense – sometimes creates a barrier to understanding what people are going through when they have a condition like Anxiety or Depression. Is there anything you can share on what it feels like to have Anxiety?

RAJ MARIWALA: It's hard to describe. Sometimes the easiest way to describe it is that my mind cannot be still, that it is overrun and overloaded with thoughts. That Anxiety is what can wake you up, or stop you from sleeping, or accompany you into dreams. In terms of physical symptoms, of course I've had everything from throwing up, breaking into a sweat, shortness of breath, digestion issues. But, also, an inability to focus, exhaustion, a need to fidget while doing some work. It can manifest as claustrophobia, feeling trapped even as one has their mask on (Covid). There are ripples of unease that run through your body reaching the tips of your fingers and toes. The usual 'solutions' – meditation, etc. make me even more agitated.

SHARE YOUR THOUGHTS

PART THREE

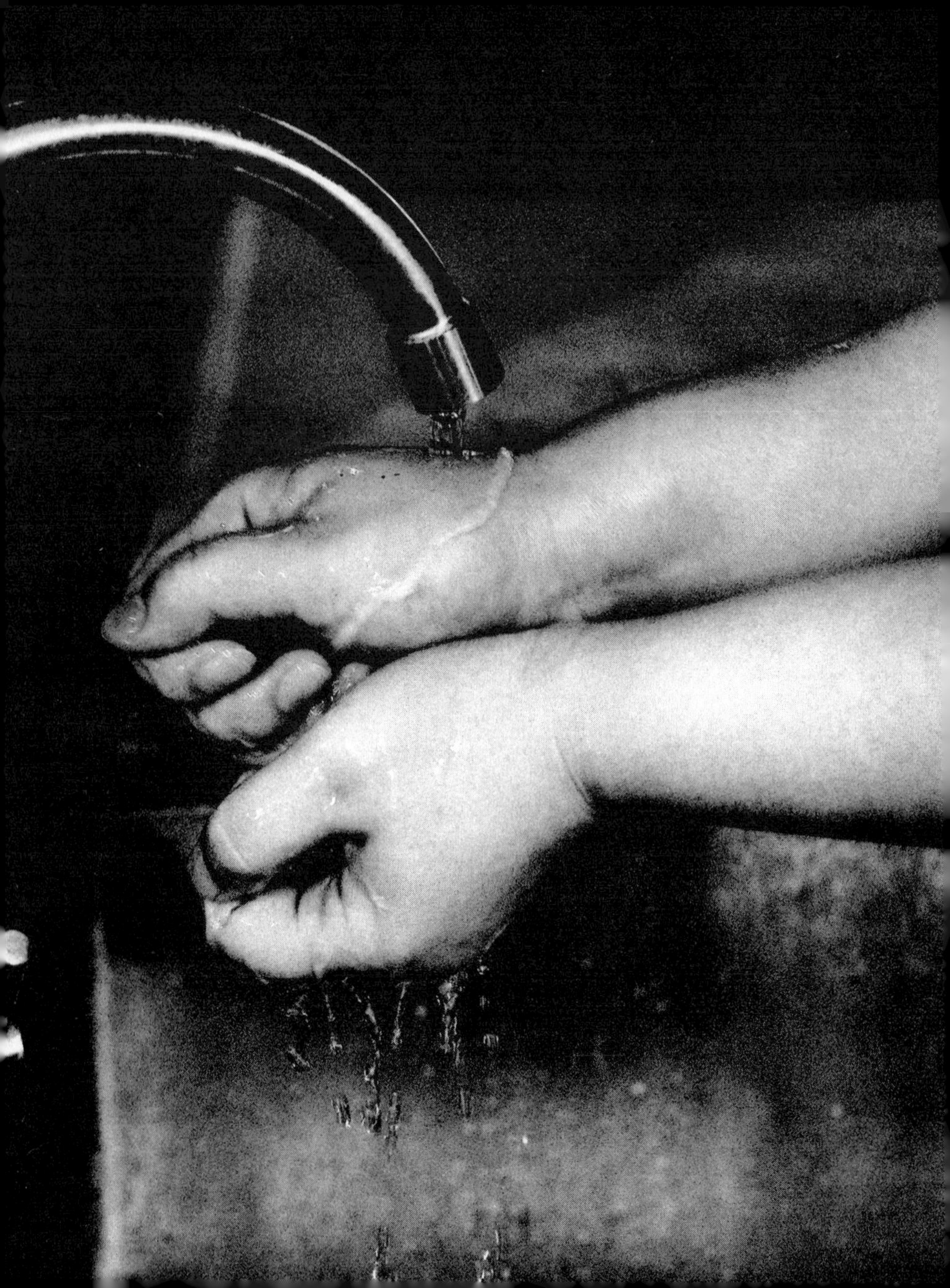

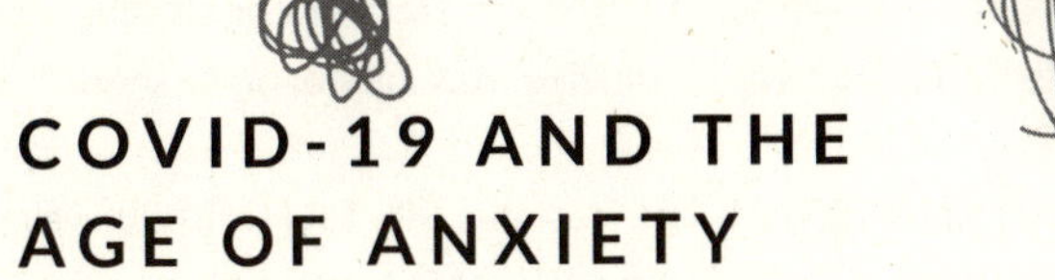

COVID-19 AND THE AGE OF ANXIETY

An Interview with Manoj Chandran

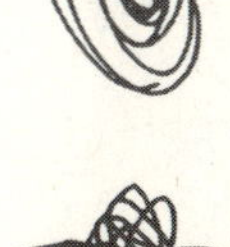

Manoj Chandran is the Founding CEO of White Swan Foundation, a non-profit organisation that empowers people with the knowledge of mental health so that they make informed decisions. At http://www.whiteswanfoundation.org, White Swan Foundation delivers India's largest knowledge repository on mental health.

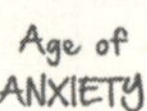

AMRITA: What are some of the key statistics or studies on Anxiety in India, that you would like to comment on or share?

MANOJ CHANDRAN: The National Mental Health Survey 2016 points out that more than 10% of the population suffers from common mental health issues, which include Anxiety. Mental health professionals agree that a significant number of people, across profiles, experience Anxiety as a clinical condition.

The White Swan Foundation portal, which receives more than a million page views a year, had 'what is anxiety' and 'anxiety disorder' among the top 10 search terms in 2019–20. During the first full quarter of COVID-19, that is the period April 1, 2020 to June 30, 2020, 'anxiety symptoms' and 'anxiety attack' were among the top 5 search terms on the portal. Besides, among the queries we receive on our social media pages and in our email inbox, anxiety is among the most popular subjects.

AMRITA: Do you think that we are living in an Age of Anxiety (disclaimer: the title of the book!); if so, why? And if not, why not?

MANOJ CHANDRAN: Even without the clinical lens, I can say that we are certainly living in the Age of Anxiety. I recall my younger days when people from the older generation would be heard using the word 'worry'. These days, it has lost the charm

and is not used much. Because, 'worry' has taken bigger (in intensity) and longer (in its period of existence) proportions. Hence, we do not seem to be satisfied with the word 'worry' in defining our condition. Though 'anxiety' is a word that should be used by mental health professionals, the word has found its way into the lexicon of the common person, because we believe that 'anxiety' better defines our experience than 'worry'. Its usage is now pervasive.

There are numerous facts in front of us to believe that we are indeed living in the Age of Anxiety.

- If you want the triggers as evidence, look at the headlines of our newspapers or the 'news' that is offered to us (not to speak of the way it is delivered) on the TV. As if we are constantly seeking information/news that creates anxiety in us and not those that relax our mind and makes us feel nice.
- Living conditions: The cities we have built are anxiety-infusing with their bursting-at-the-seams infrastructure.
- Uncertainties: Despite the best of technology and other kinds of expertise that we have with us today, we seem to be constantly living in an age of high degree of uncertainty. The pandemic has only made it worse. Mental health experts will tell us that long periods of uncertainty is not good for our brain as they may develop into Anxiety (or other forms of mental health issues).
- High degree of self-expectations: Socially, professionally and economically, we seem to be pushing ourselves to undue degree of expectations.
- Shrinking time: An hour 30 years ago used to be longer than the hour we currently have.

While these are reasons why we find ourselves in the grip of anxiety, we cannot ignore the fact that many of us are experiencing Anxiety as a mental health

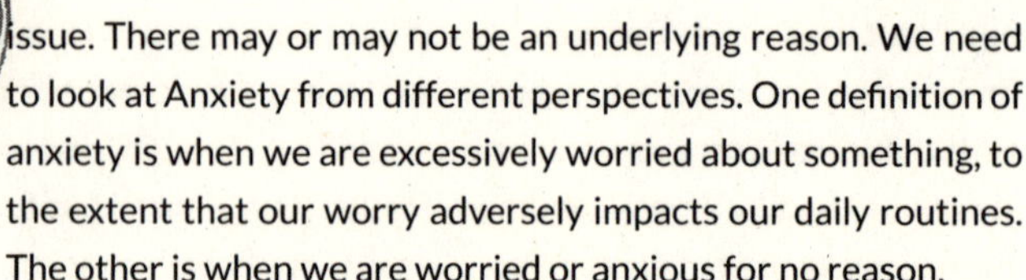

issue. There may or may not be an underlying reason. We need to look at Anxiety from different perspectives. One definition of anxiety is when we are excessively worried about something, to the extent that our worry adversely impacts our daily routines. The other is when we are worried or anxious for no reason.

AMRITA: The pandemic, lockdown 1.0, un-lockdown and many aspects have led to an uptick in mental distress, stress, anxiety and fear. Can you share any of your thoughts on this, does it reflect what you're seeing or hearing? Any specifics based on the workshops and work you're doing (e.g., with corporates).

MANOJ CHANDRAN: The pandemic and the subsequent lockdown that forced drastic changes in our social life have laid bare our lack of focus on mental health. The firm denial that we carried in our minds about mental health issues and our ignorance on the need to be emotionally prepared for such adverse situations stood exposed. Clearly, there has been a sharp increase in mental health issues such as Anxiety, Depression, loneliness and stress during the pandemic. They have manifested in situations such as our relationships at home, professional spaces and our physiological health.

When we come out of the pandemic, it would be difficult to measure the damage the recent social changes have caused on our mental health. Mental health experts point out that long periods of stress, anxiety, sadness or such emotions can result in clinical mental health issues.

Organisations have begun to realise the stressful situations their employees are working in – be it working from home or coming to office despite the pandemic. Some of them are reaching out to design programmes that help educate their employees on the need to focus on mental wellbeing and follow best practices to build emotional resilience.

AMRITA: Given how apocalyptic 2020 has been, what are some specific concerns (medium-to-long term) that you would like to highlight around Mental Health/ Mental Illness for India?

MANOJ CHANDRAN: The recent events have exposed how ill-prepared we are in dealing with adverse situations. Even as the services infrastructure for mental healthcare in India needs urgent ramping up, I am more concerned about the weakness of our social infrastructure and the lack of focus on mental well-being. The decisions we make and the situations we put ourselves in – individually or collectively – do not take into account potential risks to our mental health. They constantly expose our ignorance of the subject.

The lockdown, social stigma of being infected by the virus, the manner in which online classes were launched – while they all potentially impact our mental health, there has not been any attempt to address the same. The number of deaths due to suicide that were related to the pandemic across the country is a case in point.

Secondly, the pandemic (and the subsequent lockdown) is a clarion call to us on the need to focus on our mental health and build emotional resilience so that we are better prepared to cope with similar situations in the future. I am concerned if we have learnt any lessons. Our leaders, health experts, leaders in

organizations and social influencers must take up the responsibility of ushering the necessary mindset shift in the society to achieve this. We cannot rely on services infrastructure to address rising cases of mental health issues. Prevention would be a better solution in the long run.

AMRITA: What are some pointers you'd like to share with others — employers, employees and those who are dealing with layoffs at this stage? Any resources you'd like to share?

MANOJ CHANDRAN: Workplaces can be a great starting point in the social environment to bring about a mindset shift on mental health. Given that they have captive audiences and the fact that the leaders at workplaces can affect mindset shifts, we should work towards increasing awareness on mental healthcare here.

The key responsibility in bringing about this mindset shift lies with the leaders. Senior management and corporate leaders must own up to the need to focus on employee mental health. They must accept the fact that a significant number of their employees could possibly be suffering from mental health issues but cannot seek help due to the absence of a supportive social environment. Secondly, they must have the right knowledge of the subject to know that the greater challenges of mental healthcare lie in the social spaces and not in the clinical or services areas. It makes perfect business sense to make employee mental health one of the top strategic priorities of

organizations.

On the part of the employees, they must seek the right social environment at workplaces that furthers their idea of mental well-being and offers support and care without the fear of adverse reactions from the organisation. Employees must also have the right knowledge of their responsibilities in creating the right social environment for their co-workers who may be experiencing emotional distress. They must acquire the right knowledge to be able to play the powerful role of mental health allies.

During our professional life, we should be prepared to face several challenging situations. From incompatible bosses to challenging roles, from an uncertain professional future to job layoffs, there would be situations that will test not only our professional capabilities but also emotional resilience. With a looming recession, the pandemic has thrown a huge challenge on the working class across industries. We must be prepared to cope with the challenge with the right mental health.

Here are some useful tips, particularly on layoffs.

On Anxiety in the context of layoffs, you can check out some of our articles *Coping with Stress and Anxiety after a Layoff,*[20] *How Can my Organisation Support Employees During Layoffs,*[21] *I got Laid Off and Now I feel Hopeless.*[22]

There are many more knowledge pieces on the portal on the subject of managing Anxiety. However, remember that the decision to seek a solution to the situation should be ours. The resolve, commitment and discipline must come from within, be it the person with lived experience, their caregiver or a mental

health ally.

AMRITA: When we look at queries that White Swan Foundation receives, do you notice any differences or trends in different languages?

MANOJ CHANDRAN: Nearly 60% of content consumption on our portal takes places on our non-English language pages. Most visitors to our regional languages come from smaller towns. One possible reason could be that there are not enough mental health professionals in smaller towns. Consequently, they search for information on disorders and the treatment for the same. However, our English-speaking audience come from urban geographies and are more curious to get answers to their questions that go beyond treatment, disorders and mental health professionals.

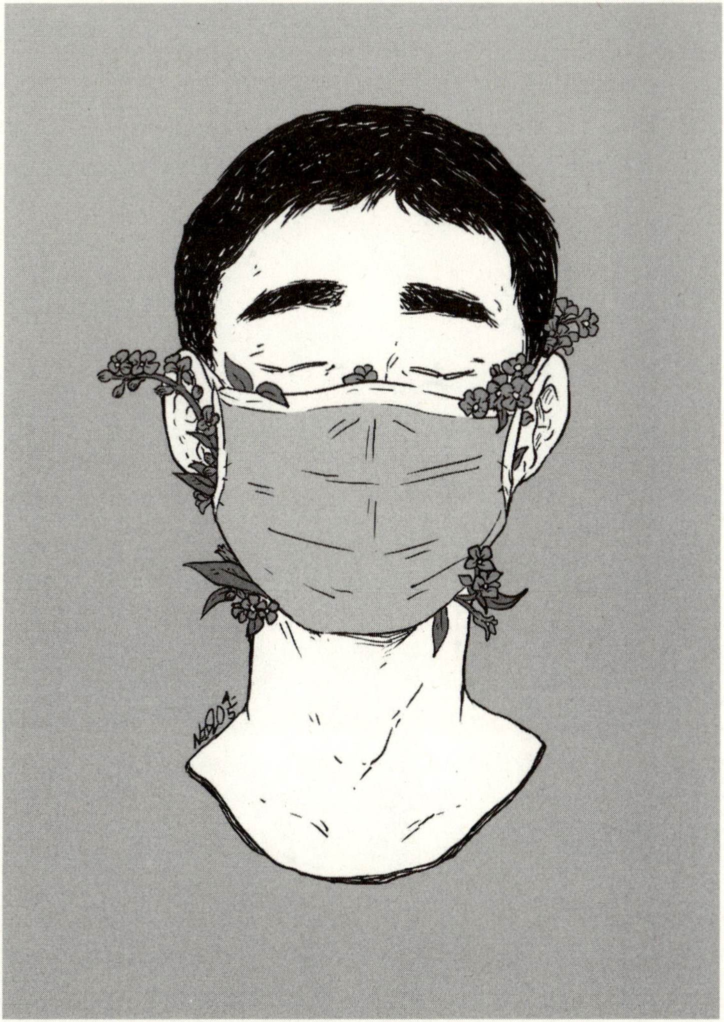

Source: Unsplash, United Nations COVID-19 Response

COVID-19, THE NEWS AND ANXIETY

By Kamna Chhibber

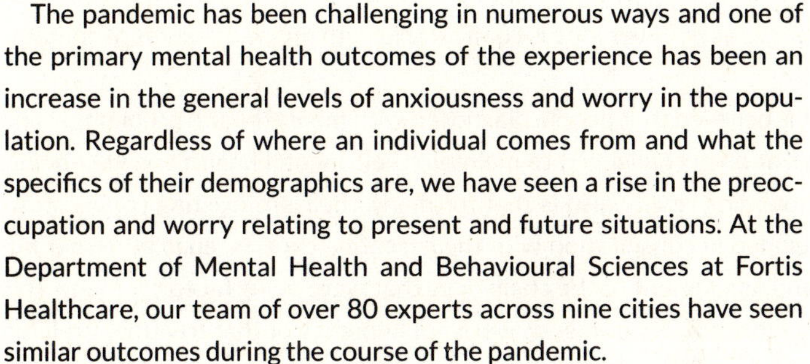

The pandemic has been challenging in numerous ways and one of the primary mental health outcomes of the experience has been an increase in the general levels of anxiousness and worry in the population. Regardless of where an individual comes from and what the specifics of their demographics are, we have seen a rise in the preoccupation and worry relating to present and future situations. At the Department of Mental Health and Behavioural Sciences at Fortis Healthcare, our team of over 80 experts across nine cities have seen similar outcomes during the course of the pandemic.

When we look at the impact the pandemic is having on the levels of anxiety, we need to consider two scenarios. The first relates to those who have already been having mental health related illness concerns and the second relates to those who find themselves struggling to maintain their mental health on account of the diverse situations that have emerged in their life.

CHALLENGES FOR THOSE WITH PRE-EXISTING CONDITIONS

Individuals with pre-existing mental health conditions have been experiencing difficulties on multiple accounts. A part of the problem originally related to maintaining continuity of treatment. Typically for mental health related problems contact with the treating experts happens at a certain frequency and the initial Anxiety for many stemmed from the challenges of maintaining this frequency, especially when the lockdown was announced. The advent and promotion of utilisation of online virtual platforms acted as a boon, supporting the treatment needs of innumerable individuals, ensuring that outreach is extended on account of the access that was provided. However, despite this for many the inability to be able to meet their treating experts in the physical realm has had its own challenges as not everyone is comfortable with online mediums of contact.

While it is believed that people diagnosed with mental health problems found themselves at once challenged to maintain their mental health and well-being, the corresponding reality also is that for many, their pre-existing coping strategies developed in consultation with their treating experts, enabled better adaptation and adjustment to the challenges that were being faced for many. This is not to say that anxiety or moods were not impacted or that treatment related challenges did not exist. These most certainly persisted as well and there was a strong need to reinforce and work towards maintaining mechanisms that facilitate coping.

During this period like all others, those with mental health related illnesses have been struggling to cope with the loneliness and isolation that have emerged on account of the lack of social connectivity. Additionally, challenges which might have existed in the personal spheres in the context of relationships too

saw an exacerbation during this period. Maintaining work–life balance has been difficult and there have been difficulties experienced on account of reductions in salaries and loss of jobs. Most importantly the ambiguity that surrounds the future has been challenging where they have had to make a significant concerted effort to keep pushing themselves to remain in the present and not allow the fears and apprehensions of the future outcomes to disrupt their lives.

CHALLENGES FACED BY THE POPULATION AT LARGE

The mental health sequelae that have resulted on account of the pandemic have first and foremost challenged individual's notions of what is 'normal'. Having to redefine this very basic aspect of their existence has in itself created substantial challenges for most. At the bottom of this lies the premise that we do not like change. Constancy and predictability is what human beings strive for and when these variables are difficult to imbibe it challenges us on far more levels than we can fathom. It creates immense restlessness, worry and anxiety within us and makes us feel unhinged. The uncertainty of what will be and how things will shape up, not having time frames in front of us that allow us to know when the next change cycle will emerge that will allow us to fall back on that which was familiar have enhanced levels of distress for most.

Concurrently, over the years reliance on social networks, being outdoors and immersing the self in activities which largely incorporate others have led to a deterioration in the comfort that people might have had in being on their own. As a result, this pandemic has challenged people's abilities to be self-reliant and engage in methods of coping and self-care that did not include or involve the presence of others or going out. Finding mechanisms for maintaining a sense of balance and relaxation has been difficult, requiring people to challenge their own inherent ways of responding to situations.

Most importantly, what has perhaps been greatly challenging is accepting that feeling anxious and worried in the current scenario where great uncertainty and ambiguity surrounds us is a need of the hour. It is only through acceptance that we can work towards maintaining coping and building resilience. This has had an impact across age groups and the expansiveness of the impact has been seen in the significant increase that has been seen in calls on helplines. The Department of Mental Health and Behavioural Sciences at Fortis Healthcare runs a free 24x7 helpline (+918376804102) which is available in 16 national languages and we have seen that there has been a substantial rise in the number of calls that are received.

In the calls we receive, people share substantial concerns about coping with the current situations that face them which have been impacting their well-being. Prominent concerns that have continually emerged range from concerns around family-related situations, to workplace anxiety, to managing and maintaining a balance between diverse roles and also attempting to ensure that they are being able to take care of their own selves. Concerns have come about which relate to the well-being of family members, particularly those who stay far away and are in the vulnerable population. The uncertainty about future outcomes have increased people's levels of stress and feelings of vulnerability. This compromises their sense of security and makes them feel out of control of the situations of their lives.

SOME STEPS TO COPE WITH ANXIETY RELATING TO COVID-19

There are some aspects that need to be particularly emphasised during this period of COVID-19 which can be helpful in coping with the situations that emerge and compromise people's sense of emotional and psychological well-being:

1. Acceptance of the current situations is a key. Fighting the reality of a situation and failing to recognise that things are the way they are takes away from a person's ability to adapt and cope with what is there in the present.

2. Reminders to the self that the situations which surround us require that we all collectively work together to combat the situations that face us is important.

3. It is essential that one recognise the temporariness of the situation and instead of projecting oneself too much into the future, try to stay in the present and work through the things that emerge one day at a time.

4. Grounding yourself in the current scenarios is a must and attempting to look at working on and solving for the problems that exist in the here and now is the right way forward.

5. Staying connected with people that you love and even those who you may not have spoken to in a long time would be helpful in maintaining some sense of normalcy. This social connectedness allows for a sense of grounding and feeling of belonging which facilitates mental well-being.

6. Reframing the thoughts that lead to anxiety is important for creating a perspective that allows for the integration of accurate and realistic aspects of the situation.

7. Reduce the information that you are consuming relating to current situations if they lead to anxiousness. Make sure whatever information you are consuming is from reliable and credible sources.

8. Focus on your own self by bringing in activities that allow you to relax and

ANXIETY IS NORMAL

BE GRATEFUL

CREATE

DANCE

EXERCISE

FANCY DRESS

GARDEN

HELP BY DONATING

IDENTIFY A QUIET PLACE

KNIT

LEARN TO PLAY AN INSTRUMENT

MEDITATE

NAP TO RELAX

JUGGLE

OPEN UP TO SOMEONE

READ

SING

PHONE A FRIEND

QUALITY TIME

VISUALIZE

UNPLUG

THIS TOO SHALL PASS

It is important to be aware and take care of your mental health during this pandemic.

WATCH YOUR FAVOURITE MOVIE

YOU ARE NOT ALONE

WE ARE IN THIS TOGETHER

THINGS TO DO TO AVOID THE BLUES

Source: Unsplash, United Nations COVID-19 Response

contribute towards making you feel a sense of calm.

9. Avoid constantly searching for more information online about the anxiety or worries that you may be having. In its place if things are getting too difficult to manage, choose to speak with experts who can help you understand what is happening.

10. Ultimately, it is important to know and remember every individual has their own unique way of coping with situations and you need to discover the way that works best for you. Do not compare or attempt to adopt the mechanisms that might be working for others. Try to find combinations of activities that work best for you.

WHAT TO DO WHEN THE NEWS TRIGGERS ANXIETY

This piece first[23] appeared in *The Health Collective.*

Anxiety is an adaptive response, an indication being provided by our mind and body to protect us from a difficult and threatening situation. In olden eras, the threat may have been posed by wild animals and fires or storms. In today's day and age, the threats can be multi-fold: it's not just about threats to our lives or livelihoods, or the threat of resources being robbed or us suffering accidents, but also much of what is going on in the world around us, through the often-apocalyptic news we see.

We are exposed to and bombarded by an enormous amount of news and information, not just every day but almost every second. **The technological shifts and the ease of access to information through the internet and social media have brought the world into our homes, continuously forcing us to stare into the face of realities that we sometimes don't understand, can't wrap our heads**

around, make sense of, or determine ways to combat and work through.

This, more often than not, causes us to feel unsettled, restless and uncertain about where things are headed. The more the sense of ambiguousness in situations rises the more difficult it becomes for us to continue without being impacted by them. This impact could be on our moods, our levels of anxiety, sleep, appetite, thinking about the world and the future or even on our perceptions of threat in the environment around us. This makes it imperative that we seek ways in which we can protect ourselves, be realistic in the interpretations we are making of the information coming our way and also take care of our health and well-being. Let's take a look at some of the things that can be and needs to be done by us towards this end.

1. **Choose what and how much you expose yourself to** – Not everyone needs to know everything or be informed about everything. It is okay for you to choose what kind of information you expose yourself to. If there are certain things that make you more anxious or cause your mood to shift then you can choose avoiding exposure to them.
2. **Be aware of the source you seek information from** – Ensure that you inform yourself about things from credible sources. Checking for the veracity of the source of the information is very important and it is essential that you be aware of the purpose behind the way media messages are created and if there could be alternate ways of looking at them or different ways in which they can be interpreted instead of being stuck with the perspective that media messages themselves are directing you towards.
3. **Know there are no expectations to be informed** – With the number of mediums available to procure news and information, we often feel pressured with the expectation to know things. It is okay if you are not aware or choose to not be

aware of certain types of information. There is no pressure to be as informed as another friend or colleague who you may be unconsciously or even consciously comparing yourself to.

4. **Get off social media if it is triggering you** – If you feel triggered by the type or amount of information and news coming your way about certain topics then feel comfortable to get off social media for a while or to block out that particular type of information. You can also make a decision to restrict your usage of the platforms to ensure that you do not feel triggered. It is important that you introduce yourself to topics that may be difficult to your pace and when you are ready for them.

5. **Take care of yourself by engaging in self-care** – An often loosely used concept, self-care nevertheless is very important. This in the context of feeling triggered would translate into knowing what things work for you and what do not. Attempt to integrate the things that make you feel more relaxed into your routine besides avoiding those that are leaving you feeling triggered.

6. **Keep sharing thoughts and feelings** – There would be numerous thoughts and feelings coursing through your mind and body during this period of time. Don't hesitate in reaching out and sharing with those you are close to. This could be a friend, family member, colleague or a professional you consult. Talking about things can help diffuse the thoughts and also help process things as one speaks about them. It also permits the processing of the emotional experiences and allows you to feel more settled and a little at ease with yourself and situations.

7. **Seek help** – If you continue to feel unsettled and it disrupts your routine, work life, social relationships and despite your efforts you do not find it settling down, then seek professional help. With the support and guidance of an expert you would be able to determine more individually specific things that could be helpful in managing your anxiety, triggers and also aid in continuing your work and relationships with greater ease.

You do not need to demonstrate strength and grit at all times. It is always important to remember that you can consider ways of removing things that are not working for you and instead act as triggers. You can choose to do things at a pace that is comfortable for you. Don't push yourself to forcibly cope with situations that are turning out to be difficult.

Source: Unsplash, United Nations COVID-19 Response

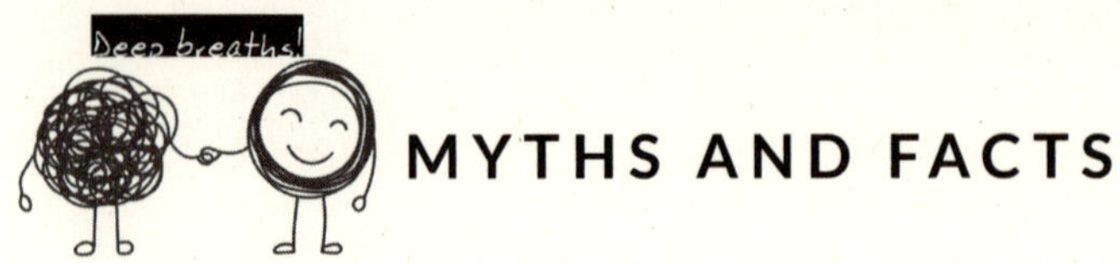

MYTHS AND FACTS

Pragya Lodha is a Clinical Psychologist, based in Mumbai. She works with eight organisations, nationally and internationally, in different capacities. She shared some Myths and Facts with Sukanya Sharma for The Health Collective *and readers of this book.*

MYTH: Having coffee / caffeine causes Anxiety

FACT: Having moderate amounts of 3–4 servings of coffee (not more than 400 mg) is normal. If a person is suffering from Anxiety disorder, having excess caffeine can aggravate the Anxiety at times but does not necessarily cause Anxiety in the first place.

MYTH: A person who has panic attacks is just faking it to get attention

FACT: This is not true, panic attacks are real with physiological, physical and emotional changes in the person who experiences panic attacks.

MYTH: AVOIDING PLACES THAT MAKE YOU FEEL ANXIOUS CAN TREAT ANXIETY

FACT: Though initially avoiding places that trigger Anxiety / panic is okay, avoiding the stressor is not the solution but actually reinforces Anxiety. Learning to unlearn the fear associated with the stressor is helpful.

MYTH: Some people are just anxious as personalities and no one can help them

FACT: That is not true, though some people have a tendency or predisposition to be more anxious than others, therapy can help them reduce their worrisome nature.

MYTH: One myth common to both Depression and Anxiety is about psychiatric medication

FACT: People think taking medication will make them addicted and/or dependent on it, but it is not true. The only point to note is that it takes a little longer to wean off psychiatric medication, but it is definitely not addictive. It is helpful to follow your doctor's advice well.

TREATMENT, SELF-CARE AND GETTING HELP

By Kamna Chhibber

First things first, we must caution you against self-diagnosis. It's very easy (and often the case!) to read a bunch of symptoms and decide they apply to you. Please don't do this! If you're concerned that you or someone close to you may have symptoms that you've read about here, do reach out to an expert for help.

Anxiety is a condition that you can learn to manage (especially with some help), and treat with the right guidance from experts.

• TREATMENT FOR ANXIETY

Anxiety Disorders affect 1 in 10 individuals and it is important to recognise that whereas experiencing anxiety or worry is normal, it is an adaptive response in most stressful and difficult situations and can affect any individual, there are numerous treatment options that are available which can enhance and improve the quality of life and mental well-being of individuals. People often hesitate on account of being uninformed, misinformed or due to the various myths and misconceptions that do surround these treatment options. However, it is imperative that you recognise that restoring the quality of life of an individual is extremely important and delaying treatment usually leads to an exacerbation of symptoms over time.

The two primary approaches that do exist with regards to treatment include psychiatric interventions utilising medication, and therapeutic interventions which employ various psychological mechanisms to help an individual develop strategies, work on thoughts and feelings, states and coping mechanisms that allow them to restore the normalcy of functioning.

'There are numerous effective methodologies that can be utilised to treat Anxiety Disorders and typically a combination of medical intervention along with psychotherapeutic intervention is utilised to gain the best treatment outcomes,' says Dr Samir Parikh, psychiatrist and Director of Department of Mental Health and Behavioural Sciences, Fortis Healthcare. 'The challenge lies more in the poor awareness pertaining to the signs and symptoms of the illness, as well as the difficulty that most individuals experience in being able to differentiate between the day-to-day anxiousness that is experienced in living a normal life and what constitutes an illness. Developing this understanding by equipping people with the right information and knowledge is a must so that people feel encouraged to reach out and seek help and intervention for illnesses like Anxiety Disorders which can very much be treated.'

• UNDERSTANDING THERAPY

Therapy involves the provision of mental health care using therapeutic modalities by a trained individual in a structured, professional setting where the idea is to help the individual in removing, modifying or retarding the existing symptoms of the illness. Additionally, an attempt is made to mediate the disturbed patterns of behaviour and also to promote positive personality growth and development.

The focus in therapy can involve the behaviour that is displayed, the thoughts that affect, the emotions that build up, the past experiences that may have contributed towards the development of the symptoms, the relational patterns that may have had a role to play as well as the current motivations and future prospects that can either be a source of distress or can result from the resolution of the symptoms.

Depending upon the type of therapeutic paradigm that is adopted the focus of the interventions can involve:

- Underlying assumptions and belief patterns
- Dysfunctional patterns of thinking
- Problematic ways of behaving or responding to situations
- Exploring and improving relationships
- Developing ways of working through problems
- Finding strategies to cope effectively

- Learning goal setting
- Maintaining optimism and building resilience

As you will have read through our interviews and first-person stories, there are numerous therapeutic approaches that can be adopted when working with someone who has an Anxiety Disorder. These include the following:

1. **Cognitive Behaviour Therapy (CBT)** – The focus in CBT is usually on challenging and changing unhelpful cognitive distortions and the behaviours that are disrupting functionality. In addition, the therapist facilitates the enhancement of emotion regulation skills, while also helping the person develop healthy coping strategies. This is all in order to facilitate or to help the person resolve the issues they are experiencing in their current circumstances.

2. **Rational Emotive Behaviour Therapy (REBT)** – REBT focuses upon helping individuals change their unhealthy, irrational beliefs which mediate difficult or maladaptive behaviours. The therapist looks to utilise problem solving techniques, cognitive restructuring techniques as well as coping techniques to enhance adaptation and help in the alleviation of the symptoms.

3. **Acceptance and Commitment Therapy (ACT)** – ACT helps and encourages individuals to embrace their thoughts and feelings. The idea is to build acceptance instead of fighting or resisting the emotional and cognitive experience that the individual is having. ACT often pairs with mindfulness-based practices and these in combination with commitment and behaviour change strategies are utilized to increase psychological flexibility.

4. **Exposure based interventions** – The premise of exposure-based therapies

such as systematic desensitisation, flooding, in vivo exposure, to name a few, involves the exposure to a feared object or stimulus to gain mastery through repeated exposure by gaining an increasing sense of control over the situation and thus over the anxiety.

5. **Psychodynamic Therapy** – Psychodynamic psychotherapy is a relatively unstructured therapeutic modality in which the past is explored to achieve insight into present problems and the ways in which these can be managed in the best way. The focus is on exploring the distressing thoughts and feelings to develop an understanding of existing patterns and defences.

Choosing which therapeutic modality might work for you can be difficult as determining the best fit and which would be the most appropriate for you can be challenging. It is most important that if you notice that you or someone you know are having signs and symptoms that indicate the presence of an Anxiety Disorder you connect to an expert who would then be able to help you determine what the best approach might be for you.

☺ ☺ ☺

SELF-CARE

A version of this section[24] first appeared in *The Health Collective*.

People go through diverse experiences and these can have an impact on each person in its own unique way. Discovering and developing mechanisms that allow for improved adaptation and enhanced coping with the prevailing situations is an imperative. One of the most important aspects that pertains to this is self-care. Self-care is often misconstrued as being selfish – the need to care for the self can be misconstrued as not being interested in or in fact, being averse to the care of another.

Busting this thought process is very important as a first step when we consider self-care. It is important to keep in mind that in caring for your own self you are not being selfish, instead you are putting in place methodologies that allow you to more effectively cope with the varying vicissitudes of your life. At the same time, these allow for the creation of both an emotional and mental space to be able to provide the help and support for another person who might be struggling with a problem of their own.

In this section we try to look at some of the strategies and mechanisms that you can incorporate in your routines, ways of thinking and doing things, which would allow you to manage your own anxiety and worries in an effective manner.

But before we go towards looking at some more specific aspects, here are some general things to keep in mind when you consider self-care:

1. **Allow yourself to experience emotions** – You are likely to feel a strong need to contain and curtail how you are feeling. People often find it difficult to stay with their emotional experiences in such situations and attempt to take steps to actively steer themselves away from them. That in reality is unhelpful and only serves to allow the distress to simmer internally. In its place accept your emotions and allow yourself to experience what is created within you spontaneously.
2. **Carve out time and space for things that make you happy and do them for yourself** – Many of us remain trapped in the circle of doing for others, pleasing others and living in accordance with what others want. Somewhere along the

way we lose sight of what makes us happy. The things that give us a feeling of calm and contentment is what we need to drift towards. This doesn't need to be in opposition to what you may be doing for others. However, carving out time and space for yourself is important.

3. **Identify your triggers and work towards developing an effective mechanism to manage them** – Some things can be more bothersome for us than others. It helps to know and identify the things which trigger us so that we can develop a way of avoiding, distracting or managing the same. It is when you feel overwhelmed and things don't seem to relent that they can overpower you and impact the way you think about yourself and your life. Working consciously to develop coping and problem solving methods would stand you in good stead.

4. **Be expressive and share** – Do not bottle up and keep your feelings within you. Allowing them to fester inside is detrimental and is likely to affect your moods and functioning across different domains of your life. Find ways of expressing your distress. Share your experience with those around you. You can seek refuge in your friends, family or colleagues.

5. **Obtain information in a thoughtful manner** – Be kind to yourself and do not push to obtain more information that is causing a heightening of your levels of distress. Be thoughtful in how much you want to know. Remember that it is acceptable for you to not seek information if it leads to disturbances in your moods or negatively impacts your thoughts and well-being.

6. **Mindfully curate the mediums you expose yourself to** – Be careful in selecting the sources from which you are seeking information. Mindfully choose those which are less triggering for you. It is not necessary for you to emulate others. Every individual has their own thresholds of distress tolerance and it is important that you be cognizant of yours to be able to maintain your relationships, your functionality and the quality of your life.

7. **Choose to disengage and disconnect** – As situations and experiences get

overwhelming make a conscious choice to disconnect and disengage from what is disturbing you. In its place expose yourself to elements which you find soothing and relaxing. Be sure to integrate these into your routines in order to keep yourself calm.

8. **Do not confuse self-care with selfishness** – It is easy to become overly judgmental about prioritising yourself and view the steps you are taking in a negative light. Be careful to not label yourself as being selfish and non-empathetic or non-sympathetic because you need to care for yourself. To be able to support another and to fully understand their experiences you need to feel fully well yourself.

9. **Connect to your loved ones and build a support system** – Nothing is more important than having a solid support system around you. This can include your friends, family, colleagues and co-workers. Having a supportive network of people around you can help you feel comforted, certain that someone would be there in case you're feeling troubled, and sure that they would pull you out of a negative spiral if it is required.

10. **Never hesitate to take help from a professional** – If you find yourself dipping in your moods, feeling uncertain about where you are at or where you are heading, if life seems purposeless or you feel that you are increasingly unsure of yourself and your relationships, reach out for help. The stigma is in our minds. And finding the answers and support in an expert can be the right step if you are struggling. Reach out for help by calling on a helpline or connecting with a psychiatrist or psychologist for in-person interactions.

Taking care of yourself will go a long way in you also being able to help those around you. Self-care has no substitute.

DEEP-DIVE: TAKING CARE OF YOURSELF IF YOU HAVE ANXIETY

1. Know What Worries You

The first step towards self-care involves developing a robust understanding of what it is that worries you. Often you might find yourself in a space where you struggle to define exactly what may be troublesome or difficult. This in itself can be a significant contributor towards your anxiety. Not being able to identify, define or describe your source of worry or anxiety can create a feeling of substantive apprehension and vulnerability that can be rather difficult to cope with. As a result, one of the first things that you must attempt to do in a situation where you find yourself plagued by worries and anxiety is to try and develop an understanding of where the worry is coming from.

You must keep in mind that your Anxiety does not need to necessarily come from a singular source. More often than not, people tend to have multiple things going on in their life – some real and others imagined on account of what they perceive might have happened or could happen – that tend to be a substantial cause for the Anxiety that they experience. Thus, it is imperative before you do anything else, you make a concerted and proactive effort to try and determine the source of this anxiety or worry.

Often times these aspects can seem irrational and illogical or you might think that they are too trivial and should be immediately discarded. In some instances you would be able to do so but yet for many others the thoughts and feelings would persist which make you feel that anxiety and worry is percolating through your mind and body. Give attention to these even if they feel trivial or others around you point them to be minor concerns that can be easily ignored, avoided or even altered.

What bothers you and affects you is important. Acknowledging and accepting this will also allow you to actively problem solve for these and move in a direction of being able to put in place strategies that allow you to cope with them.

2. **Some Tips for Relaxation**

People often confuse relaxation with engaging in extensive practices to combat stress and Anxiety. There are numerous simple things that can be indulged in to be able to relax and calm yourself and these can be effectively built into your routines to obtain the best results. Here are some things that you can consider when it comes to relaxation:

a. Breathing exercises – Simple breathing exercises can be very helpful in building relaxation when utilised regularly.
b. Meditation – Meditative practices are known to help in coping with stress, developing a positive attitude, and building resilience in the long run.
c. Music – This is an easy and effective way of promoting relaxation through the substantial benefits that it leads to in terms of overall wellness.
d. Exercise – Physical activity is a known mechanism that helps in coping with stress and allows people to find their own unique ways of relaxing. Be it rigorous physical exercise or activities like walking, running or tai chi, anything that works well for you is going to be helpful in building relaxation
e. Art activities – Art-based activities tend to have significant benefits in terms of helping people relax. These can involve the utilisation of drawing, painting, sculpting or any other mediums that you might enjoy.
f. Guided imagery – Guided imagery is often used to help individuals develop

ways of relaxing themselves.

g. Progressive muscle relaxation – This is a technique in which each muscle group is tensed and then guided to relax, making one more aware of the physical sensations that accompany feeling stressed and changing them.

3. **Steer Away from Guilt and Self-Blame**

Guilt and self-blame can often make it difficult to cope with situations. These complex emotions compromise an individual's ability to be able to adapt to the scenarios they find themselves in. In the midst of a difficult situation it is important to try and focus on what the situation demands and attempt to work with those aspects. Sticking to the tangibles of the situation would allow you to be able to steer away from guilt and self-blame.

Also ask yourself 'Given the way things are poised today what is it that you can do that will change it?'

Instead of getting stuck in a cycle of guilt and self-blame, try to find a way to push yourself to do something about what is causing you to feel these emotions.

Even when nothing can be done taking ownership of what might be making you feel the way that you are would go a long way in coping better with the situation you find yourself in. Finally, make a concerted effort to do a post-hoc analysis and understand what it was that happened in the situation to ensure that you can prevent yourself from being caught in the same cycle again.

4. **Be Your Own Cheerleader**

You might not always have people around you who would be able to help boost your confidence and belief in who you are and what you are doing. Being realistically oriented to what you do and achieve during the course of your day and life allows you to maintain a sense of positivity about how things are going for you. This does not mean that you need to blow your own trumpet and keep informing others around you of your accomplishments.

Instead this has more to do with being more self-aware so you can utilise the positivity that gets generated through these understandings and reminders to keep yourself going even when things get difficult and the outcomes are negative.

5. **Know When to Reach Out for Help**

Self-care involves also knowing when it is important for you to seek help for your own self. If you notice signs and symptoms that can be indicators towards the presence of a mental health concern or if you struggle to cope with emotions and thoughts, reach out to someone. This could be a friend or a family member or even an expert. Always remember reaching out for help is not a sign of weakness.

☺ ☺ ☺

TAKING CARE OF SOMEONE WITH ANXIETY

Understand the Illness: Hopefully reading some of the stories in this book and hearing from the person directly will help amplify your understanding of the disorder.

It takes patience and acceptance: It takes a lot of patience to care for someone with a condition. You should know that with the right coping skills (and possibly a combination of therapy and medication if required), the person will be able to find a way of working through the illness and coping with situations. It's alright of you to also unplug and take care of yourself when you need to!

The need for problem-solving skills: You'll find that learning creative problem-solving skills can be a great asset in helping someone deal with Anxiety. Try to not keep focusing on only the emotions the person is sharing in the situation and attempt to determine if there is some cause that might be at the root of the problem. Demonstrating problem-solving skills and approaches would go a long way in enabling the person in becoming self-reliant as well.

Encouraging help-seeking: There's a difference between encouraging someone to seek help and trying to force them to do so. The latter is not likely to be very helpful. Perhaps indicate examples or share stories of people who have been able to seek help, or even help shortlist people to reach out to.

Managing guilt and self-blame: It's very easy to blame yourself or feel guilty if someone you care about gets triggered or you feel that you can't help them enough. Trust the process, and be as open and accepting as you can of the situation. Guilt and self-blame will not be helpful to anyone and if you can, learn to let these go.

Keeping the anger and resentment in check: It's completely human and understandable if you get angry or start resenting the person you're caring for but if you find yourself flaring up often, you might need to take a time-out. You deserve a break too. This is why self-care for the caregiver is so important. Put your own oxygen mask on first, before you try to help anyone else, and do take a time-out if you feel that you're reacting in a volatile manner. Deep breathing and cutting yourself some slack would be important to help manage the situation. Try not to react out of anger.

Self-care for the caregiver: What are some hobbies you enjoy? Does art or music or reading help you self-soothe? Do you have something productive you want to do just for yourself? Maybe talk to a friend daily with no agenda, or try picking up something like gardening, or knitting, even colouring books can be quite stress-busting. You need to take care of yourself before you can take care of someone else, so don't think of it as something selfish or self-centred – it's essential.

HELPLINES IN INDIA

ALL-INDIA	GOVT MH Rehabil-itation HELPLINE 'KIRAN'	18005990019	24/7
ALL-INDIA	VANDREVALA FOUN-DATION	1860-266-2345	24 BY 7/ EMAIL HELP@VAN-DREVALAFOUNDATION.COM IF YOU DON'T GET THROUGH AND EXPECT A CALL-BACK
	FORTIS HOSPITAL NATIONAL HELPLINE	91-8376804102	24 by 7 / Multilingual
BANGALORE	SAHAI	080-25497777	
CHENNAI	JEEVAN SUICIDE PREVENTION HO-TLINE	044-2656 4444	
	SNEHA	044-2464 0050	EMAIL: help@snehaindia.org
DELHI	SANJIVINI SOCIETY FOR MENTAL HEALTH	24311918, 243118883	EMAIL: sanjivini1971@gmail.com
	SNEHI	9582208181	10 am to 10 pm Daily
GANGTOK	SIKKIM HELPLINE NUMBER	1800-3453225 / 03592-202111	
HYDERABAD	ONE LIFE	78930 78930	
KOCHI	MAITHRI	91-484 -2540530	
KOLKATA	SERVE	9830785060	
	DEFEAT DEPRES-SION	9830027975	
	CLIPPINGS	98300 27976	

MUMBAI	SINGING SOULZ	9892003868	
	SAMARITANS	84229 84528/ 84229 84529 / 84229 84530	3-9 PM (all days) EMAIL: talk2samaritans@gmail.com You can call and speak anonymously and confidentially, or visit the centre for a personal meeting in Mumbai, with a prior appointment. Address:402, Jasmine, Opp Kala Kendra, Dadasaheb Phalke Road, Dadar(E), Mumbai 400014
NAGPUR	Nagpur Suicide Prevention Helpline	8888817666	

Legal Disclaimer: *The Health Collective* is not in the business of nor intends to provide counselling service. The professionals, the website of the professionals and helpline numbers listed on *The Health Collective* or in this book are not employed, associated or endorsed by *The Health Collective*. The professionals and the organisations behind the listed websites and helpline numbers, on *The Health Collective* website or reproduced in this book, are independent third-parties and there is no relationship of principal-agent, employer-employee, partnership of any nature with *The Health Collective*. *The Health Collective*, the publishers of this book and the authors do not make any recommendation or guarantee service or quality of any professional or helpline number or website listed herein. *The Health Collective* does not make any representations, warranties or guarantees as to, and is in no manner responsible for, the services provided by the professionals or their websites or the helpline services. The stories and comics set out by *The Health Collective* are intended purely for reference purposes. Advice or stories set out herein are by no means intended to malign or defame any person, organisation, caste or community. Advice or stories set out herein are views of the concerned authors only, *The Health Collective* does not claim copyright or endorse or recommend or represent on veracity of the advice contained in the articles or stories (including the comics) on this website or reproduced in this book. Additionally, the articles and stories set out herein should not in any manner be considered as substitute for professional help. All experiences are personal, hence advice and suggestions contained in the articles and stories may not apply to a reader's specific facts or situations, and it is recommended that professional help is sought for such matters. *The Health Collective*, the publishers and authors disclaim all liability of all nature arising out of reliance placed on the advice set out in the stories or arising out of meetings with professionals or calls with the professionals or helpline numbers mentioned on the website of *The Health Collective* or in this book.

ACKNOWLEDGEMENTS

AMRITA

Each book in the Mindscape series has been structured slightly differently, as some of you will have seen... but it is stories of lived experience that are at the heart of each one. Your stories, our stories, count in unimaginable ways, I've come to realise. These are not easy stories to share, but they are critical. Healing is possible when we let the words in... when we let the light and the hope in.

I would like to thank each and every one of our contributors and interviewees for taking the time to be part of this mammoth endeavour. I couldn't have dreamt of pulling off a book like this without your generosity and perspective.

We stand (and sometimes rest) on the shoulders of giants — none of this would have been possible without an entire community of people who are dedicated to the idea of creating more space for these conversations in today's India, a luxury perhaps, that previous generations did not have. (And yet, I can't help thinking, so much more needs to be done.)

I want to thank my wonderful co-author Kamna, who has been a consistent mental health advocate ever since I've known her, and incredibly generous with her time and insights, despite all the chaos inherent this past year. I still well remember that first cup of coffee in a little café so many years ago, and some super helpful advice when *The Health Collective* was still a fledgling project!

Dr Bhagat, I can't thank you enough for your support throughout this journey (all our interviews, videos and conversations over the past decade and a half!) Thank you so much for your Foreword for this book, written at a particularly busy time, in a full-blown pandemic, no less.

Huge thanks to Arti, Ayushi, Girish, Ilina, Jessica, Niharika, Pragya and Rajashree, for your courage and grace, and for sharing so much with us. Thanks so much to Manoj, Raj, Dr Pathare and dear Tanmoy — it's been incredible to see how robust, important, even critical your work has been.

A huge thank you to Himanjali Sankar for dreaming up this series with me several years ago, for Rahul, Sayantan for the incredible support and belief in this project; the super-talented Mridu, Abhay and Shobhita, as well as the sales team led by Richie, who have made a heroic effort in a decidedly unusual pandemic year. Writing is far from the one-person job it's made out to be!

Sukanya, thank you for getting our Myths and Facts and colloquial terms together, with input and insight from Pragya and Dr Gautam. Amartya, thank you for the legal disclaimer and having our back! And thank you so much, patrons of *The Health Collective*!

Super dollops of thanks as always to my own support system — loved ones, mentors and friends. To those who put up with the weird and wired versions, who love the passion and zeal but aren't put off by the 'I'm-overhwhelmed-and-close-to-burning-out' phases, who will ask me once in a while to take a beat, take a break, and take care of myself. Put your own oxygen mask on first, my dear friend Vanita told me more than a decade and change ago, and she's right, of course. I hope that that advice serves some of you well too...

My final words of gratitude are for you, dear readers. Thank you for your support and for your interest in this subject — I hope that you all find something helpful in this book.

KAMNA

It has been a real pleasure collaborating and working with Amrita and our editors on this book which has been written on such a relevant and important topic, considering the times we find ourselves in.

It no doubt takes a lot of effort and hard work in bringing together not just words but people to share those words that weave an intricate narrative, creating a space that is represented by this book which not only can readers identify with, but can also gain much knowledge and information from to be able to live more fulfilling lives.

There is immense gratitude for the time that has been taken out by all the experts and individuals who have shared their personal journeys, especially given the context of this pandemic that has overtaken all our lives. Their experiential understanding and their words of wisdom will no doubt benefit all those who read this book.

I would also like to share my heart-felt gratitude towards my teachers and mentors who have been stalwarts supporting my personal and professional journey, guiding me in how to build my skills and develop the right approach towards my work. My colleagues and the clients I have worked with have provided innumerable learning opportunities as well as pushed me to enhance my skill base. It has been the cumulative benefit of these multiple experiences that has enabled me to share my understanding and knowledge with all who choose to read this book.

Endnotes

1 With thanks to Dr Soumitra Pathare, Dr Avinash De Souza, Hvovi Bhagwagar, Stuti Saxena, Dr Kersi Chavda.
2 Benjamin J. Sadock, Virginia A Sadock and Pedro Ruiz, *Kaplan & Sadock's Synopsis of Psychiatry : Behavioral Sciences/ Clinical Psychiatry*, 11th edition, (Philadelphia: Wolters Kluwer, 2015).
3 'National Mental Health Survey of India, 2015-16: Prevalence, Pattern and Outcomes', (NIMHANS, Bengaluru: 2016).
4 Arti Malik, 'Long Read, Anxiety Disorders in India', The Health Collective, 17 July 2017, (http://www.healthcollective.in/2017/07/long-read-anxiety-disorders-in-india)
5 'Depression and Other Common Mental Disorders: Global Health Estimates', Geneva: World Health Organization; 2017. Licence: CC BY-NC-SA 3.0 IGO.
6 Trivedi, J.K., & Gupta, P.K. (2010), 'An overview of Indian research in anxiety disorders', *Indian Journal of Psychiatry*, 52 (Suppl 1), S210–S218. (https://doi.org/10.4103/0019-5545.69234)
7 G. Gururaj et al, 'National Mental Health Survey of India, 2015-16: prevalence, patterns and outcomes', National Institute of Mental Health and Neuro Sciences, NIMHANS Publication No. 129 (2016).
8 'Bengaluru: Anxiety, Depression eating into Corporate India, says Study', *Deccan Chronicle*, retrieved 18 January 2021. (https://www.deccanchronicle.com/nation/current-affairs/181118/bengaluru-anxiety-depression-eating-into-corporate-india-says-study.html)
9 Girish Iyer, 'Your Stories: How I've Lived with Depression, Panic Attacks and Anxiety Disorder', The Health Collective, 16 March 2020, (http://www.healthcollective.in/2020/03/living-with-depression-panic-attacks-anxiety-disorder/)
10 Rajashree Gandhi, 'How Bullet Journal Helped me Deal With Anxiety & Why I will Never Force it On You', The Health Collective, 6 April, 2018, (http://www.healthcollective.in/2018/04/how-bullet-journal-helped-me-deal-with-my-anxiety-why-i-will-never-force-it-on-you/)
11 Evernote Team, 'Productivity in Mind: How Ryder Carroll Designed Bullet Journal', Evernote, 3 August, 2015, (https://evernote.com/blog/how-ryder-carroll-designed-bullet-journal/)
12 Jessica Xalxo, 'Your Stories: The Anxious Hat', The Health Collective, 8 April 2018, (http://www.healthcollective.in/2018/04/your-stories-the-anxious-hat/)
13 Ayushi Khemka, 'My Journey with Anxiety: No It's Not Nervousness', The Health Collective, 30 November 2020, (http://www.healthcollective.in/2020/11/my-journey-with-anxiety-no-its-not-nervousness/)
14 M.A. Crocq, 'A history of anxiety: from Hippocrates to DSM', Dialogues Clin Neurosci. 2015 Sep;17(3):319-25. (doi: 10.31887/DCNS.2015.17.3/macrocq. PMID: 26487812; PMCID: PMC4610616).
15 Graham C.L. Davey, 'Is there an Anxiety Epidemic', Psychology Today, 6 November 2018, (https://www.psychologytoday.com/us/blog/why-we-worry/201811/is-there-anxiety-epidemic)
16 Ashleigh Garrison, 'Antianxiety drugs — often more deadly than opioids — are fueling the next drug crisis in US', CNBC, 3 August 2018, (https://www.cnbc.com/2018/08/02/antianxiety-drugs-fuel-the-next-deadly-drug-crisis-in-us.html)
17 Tanmoy Goswami, 'The coronavirus is reminding us that anxiety is good – as long as it doesn't turn to panic', *The Correspondent*, 27 March 2020, (https://thecorrespondent.com/373/the-coronavirus-is-reminding-us-that-anxiety-is-good-as-long-as-it-doesnt-turn-into-panic/49379260348-64211471)
18 https://twitter.com/toymango/status/911075397235650560?s=20
19 'Data and Statistics on Children's Mental Health', Centers for Disease Control and Prevention, retrieved 24 January 2021, (https://www.cdc.gov/childrensmentalhealth/data.html)
20 Coping with stress and anxiety after a layoff', 8 January 2020, White Swan Foundation, (https://www.whiteswanfoundation.org/workplace/coping-with-stress-and-anxiety-after-a-layoff)
21 How can my organisation support employees during layoffs', 15 August 2016, White Swan Foundation, (https://www.whiteswanfoundation.org/workplace/how-can-my-organization-support-employees-during-layoffs)
22 'I got laid off and now I feel hopeless', 15 August 2016, White Swan Foundation, (https://www.whiteswanfoundation.org/workplace/i-got-laid-off-and-now-i-feel-hopeless)
23 Kamna Chhibber, 'Ask the Experts: What to Do if the News is Triggering Anxiety', 15 August, 2019, The Health Collective, (http://www.healthcollective.in/2019/08/what-to-do-if-the-news-is-triggering-anxiety/)
24 Kamna Chhibber, 'Ask the Experts: How to Care for Yourself in Tough Times', The Health Collective, 4 March 2020, (http://www.healthcollective.in/2020/03/ask-the-experts-how-to-care-for-yourself-in-tough-times/)